To Kath[...]
my cher[...]
[...] [...] love,
Jane

To my little sister — enjoy
and pass along. — Kathy
P.S. My friend Jane's story is on
pg. 61

Lori — I have enjoyed
this book and all the
blessings from reading
each story. I hope you
do too. — Linda

CELEBRATING
CHRISTMAS

COMPILED AND EDITED
BY TERRI KALFAS

GRACE

Royalties for this book are donated to Samaritan's Purse.

CELEBRATING CHRISTMAS

ISBN-13: 978-1-60495-077-9

From Samaritan's Purse

We so appreciate your donating all royalties from the sale of the books *Divine Moments, Christmas Moments, Spoken Moments, Precious Precocious Moments, More Christmas Moments, Stupid Moments, Additional Christmas Moments, Loving Moments, Merry Christmas Moments, Coolinary Moments, Moments with Billy Graham, Personal Titanic Moments, Remembering Christmas, Romantic Moments, Pandemic Moments, Christmas Stories, Broken Moments* and now *Celebrating Christmas,* to Samaritan's Purse.

What a blessing that you would think of us! Thank you for your willingness to bless others and bring glory to God through your literary talents. Grace and peace to you.

Their Mission Statement:

Samaritan's Purse is a nondenominational evangelical Christian organization providing spiritual and physical aid to hurting people around the world.

Since 1970, Samaritan's Purse has helped victims of war, poverty, natural disasters, disease, and famine with the purpose of sharing God's love through his son, Jesus Christ.

Go and do likewise
Luke 10:37

You can learn more by visiting their website at
samaritanspurse.org

Dedicated to Yvonne Lehman,

who helped bring the Divine Moments series into being,

to the writers who share our vision,

and to the readers

we hope will be blessed by our stories.

Table of Contents

Celebrating Two Advents

Lydia E. Harris

Before Christmas, my friend wrote to me, "After much prayer, I finally finished decorating our home for Christmas. It's quite different than it has ever been. We are no longer celebrating the birth of a baby. We are celebrating the soon-coming of the King, the One who 'is called Faithful and True.'" (See Revelation 19:11.)

Her note offered an exciting reminder that as we celebrate Jesus's first Advent, which means the coming of Christ, we can also anticipate His second Advent.

Although my decorating didn't change, I began listening to Christmas music in a new way. Several songs turned my heart to Christ's return as well as to His birth.

As we sang "O Holy Night" in church, tears ran down my face as I rejoiced that His first coming on that holy night meant another holy time will occur when Jesus returns. He will again come with multitudes of angels, but this time *everyone* will fall on their knees in worship. The song also speaks of Him breaking chains. I rejoiced that when Christ comes to rule, oppression will truly cease and we will praise Jesus as Lord.

One of my favorite songs in Handel's *Messiah* is "The Trumpet Shall Sound." Since I played the trumpet in school, I wait for the jubilant, brassy sound that comes in the third part of the oratorio. The lyrics include words from 1 Corinthians 15:52 (KJV): "*The trumpet shall sound, and the dead shall be raised incorruptible, and we shall be changed.*" These words stir my heart as I anticipate the Rapture. Yes, one day the trumpet will sound and Christ will return for His Bride. So, I am eagerly listening for the trumpet.

The *Messiah* also includes the magnificent "Hallelujah" chorus, which heralds such triumph and victory. It proclaims Jesus as King of kings and Lord of lords, who will reign forever and ever. That's our marvelous hope and future.

Another Christmas song that speaks of Jesus's return is "Mary, Did You Know?" One phrase stands out to me, that Jesus will rule the nations. When He returns, He will be the perfect Ruler. As we sing in "Joy to the World," He will rule with truth and grace. This familiar carol was actually written about His Second Coming, but has been adopted as a Christmas hymn.

"In the First Light" also speaks of Jesus coming back to rule the earth. It concludes by saying that this event will be even greater than His first coming. Just imagine! Jesus will return as a ruling King instead of a helpless baby.

As we celebrate Jesus's first coming, we can anticipate His second Advent. Together, in our hearts and homes, we can worship Him as the soon-coming King. And so, I pray: Lord Jesus, I love You and rejoice in Your birth. But now I long for Your return. As we again prepare our hearts for You, we eagerly pray, "Come soon, Lord Jesus."

More Than Ornaments

Suzanne D. Nichols

I sighed as I adjusted myself on the lumpy sofa in our mobile home. The Christmas issue of a popular women's magazine lay open across my lap, its colorful photographs of perfectly decorated cookies and Christmas trees enticing me from every other page. I had been thrilled when my co-worker loaned me the magazine. But, as I studied the newest holiday trends, worry chipped away at my Christmas spirit.

Soon, we'd celebrate our first Christmas as a married couple. I wanted it to be special. But, with Roger in college our budget didn't allow for many extras — certainly not the extravagant decorations featured in the magazine. I looked away from the alluring photos and attempted to rein in my imagination.

Perhaps we could buy a string of colored lights and a box of glass ornaments from Rose's Department Store.

A quick breath caught in my throat as I imagined a tall cedar tree entwined with color and hung with iridescent ornaments splashing rainbow auras onto the ceiling and walls of this long, narrow space.

Even that seemed out of reach.

Yes, funds were limited. But thankfully, Roger and I both had jobs. His was part-time, but dependable. And he was able to flex it around his classes and long study hours. My earnings as a hairstylist drawing a fifty-percent commission were less predictable.

We also considered ourselves blessed to live near my grandparents, who made sure we had vegetables from their garden and frequent invitations to evening dinners and Sunday lunches.

As clearly as they recognized our tribulations, they just as wisely guided us to develop our own ways of working shoulder to shoulder. Married less than six months, Roger and I were already making hard choices and sweet memories, working toward the goal of a rewarding career, and clinging to the promise that our college poverty would one day end.

My dreams of lovely Christmas decorations seemed as distant as that promise.

I drew a deep breath and tossed the open magazine onto the sofa. As the air slowly escaped my lips, my frustration eased and I looked over at the discarded magazine. Picking it up, I realized it had flipped to a new page.

With renewed interest, I discovered photographs of cute and crafty projects, handmade gifts and decorations. One example held my attention — ornaments made from two simple items: a Christmas card and the round end of a large plastic egg from a well-known pantyhose package. A loop of ribbon served as the hanger.

I quickly called my grandmother and asked for any Christmas cards she would allow me to plunder. Next, I scoured my sock drawer in search of the special pantyhose packages.

Surrounded by ribbon, cards, and several pantyhose eggs, I sat at my kitchen table that evening with scissors and glue in hand and the joy of Christmas growing in my heart. A collection of ornaments grew along with that joy, and when I finally sat back to examine the bounty, I surveyed a generous presentation for the branches of our yet-to-be-acquired tree.

Roger took a study break to admire my creations.

As we shared a bowl of popcorn, I showed him the miniature scenes and small-scale graphics I'd trimmed from the cards to fit each egg's smaller half. The images were glued onto a narrow ridge inside the opening. A coordinating ribbon encircled the outer edge, knotted into a generous loop at the top for hanging.

I dangled one from my index finger and gave it a half-spin.

"See how the silvery finish reflects like a mirror? I can't wait to hang these on our tree."

"I can look for one on Saturday while you're working," Roger offered.

"I would love that!" I laughed, giving him a playful pat on the cheek.

Saturday arrived with the kind of clear skies and bright sunshine that often conceal the crispness of a December morning. Roger declared it to be a perfect day and was already gearing up for the promised search as I headed off to work. He had a plan, so I left him to it, along with a reminder that a cedar would fill our little home with woodsy Christmas cheer.

When I returned home that evening, Roger had positioned his find in front of the window and was pouring water into the bowl of the stand as I walked through the door. He straightened in time to catch my questioning gaze.

It was *not* a cedar. It was, in fact, a rather sad excuse for a pine. The trunk was crooked, the branches gangly, and the needles a sickly yellow-green.

"It's the best I could do," Roger shrugged. "And it was free. I cut it off the abandoned lot across from the trailer park."

I dared not speak for fear the tears would flow.

Roger continued in a tone that bordered on insistence. "By the time we string lights through it, hang your crafty creations and maybe some candy canes, we won't even notice all . . . that." He motioned toward the tree with an outstretched palm, stopping short of naming the pitiful thing's flaws.

I softened, allowing his vision to spark my imagination. "I could make a popcorn garland and you could spray-paint pinecones."

"Perfect!" He drew me to him and kissed my temple. "I'll help you with the popcorn tonight, and we'll gather pinecones tomorrow."

I relaxed in his embrace, grateful for his enthusiasm and the glimmer of hope it brought.

During Sunday lunch with my grandparents, we shared the story of our sad-looking tree and our plans to turn it into a thing of beauty. They offered us two strands of colored lights, a handful of candy canes, and a red tablecloth for a tree skirt.

Before long, with a combination of creativity and resourcefulness, we'd fashioned a decent-looking Christmas tree. Not a thing of beauty. Certainly not magazine worthy. But as we settled onto our sofa late in the afternoon of our first Christmas day as a married couple, we held each other and marveled at our accomplishment. Not only had we been able to decorate our little home for Christmas, we had worked it out together.

As afternoon ebbed, the illuminated tree took command of the darkened room. Our silvery ornaments became convex mirrors, reflecting distorted images of candy canes, pinecones, popcorn, and lights.

In that moment, my Christmas craft born out of college poverty became more than thrifty ornaments for our lovingly transformed tree. They became a picture of marriage.

In creating an ornament, part of the card was cut away and discarded. Only one half of the egg was needed. In a similar way, when a couple marries, they choose to leave behind certain aspects of the single life, fully committing to each other. Two unique individuals give themselves to a singular endeavor: a strong and meaningful relationship. Crafted from two, their bond forms one new creation, secured with the glue of commitment, and encircled with the ribbon of unity.

I rested my head on Roger's chest, content to linger in the glimmering, comforting moment, a moment of sweet awareness that our newly-formed marriage — fashioned with care and purpose — was the ornament that made this Christmas truly special.

3

A More Silent Night

Susan Brehmer

December is not normally a relaxing month for me. As a church musician, I start the process of planning and choosing songs for the Christmas season in late October. Rehearsals begin in earnest during November. Each year our music team presents a Christmas concert, which adds to the number of songs to prepare beyond the usual Sunday worship activities. An extra rehearsal or two fill already jam-packed weeks. The season always flies by in a flurry. By the time Christmas Eve rolls around, I'm exhausted. December feels shorter every year as days rush by in a blizzard of holiday preparations and party invitations.

Not so last year.

Church gatherings moved online during the pandemic. Social distancing and restrictions on singing curtailed band rehearsals. Worship services morphed as we adjusted the format to fit what worked for people viewing from home. Noteworthy changes were fewer songs than usual, which we now recorded ahead of time for use during the scheduled services.

Because my husband worked from home during that season, finding time to record each part was challenging at times. I also needed to provide the rest of the music team enough lead time so they could record their parts while their family members were at home as well.

The process to create song videos presented a significant learning curve. As the primary instrumentalist, I rehearsed and recorded an audio version of the keyboard or guitar part. This alone presented a challenge. I had to be strategic about when I could practice or record. I could take the guitar to the other end of the house, close a door, and play without disrupting my husband's online meetings, but the piano was not so portable. I often consulted with my "new co-worker" to determine the optimal time to rehearse or record to not interfere with his business interactions. All that planning just to record the instrumental. On one particular occasion he cheerfully announced his return from running an errand just as I was playing the closing bars of a piece. I don't think you can hear his joyous greeting on the final version.

Capturing my vocal part was a much easier process. I set up a video camera at the opposite end of the house, put in my earbuds, and sang along to my piano or guitar audio track. It usually took me a few false starts to create a vocal video. One time I forgot to recharge the battery and realized I only had enough juice for one take, if that. The entire time I sang I kept looking at the indicator — which had turned red part way through — wondering if the battery charge would make it to the end of the song. Thankfully, it did because I had only had a short window of opportunity to make the recording.

While this new process presented a steep learning curve and a lot of extra work, much of the prep and polish of Christmas music occurred during the first half of December. As the month progressed, my music responsibilities decreased.

Although the process was a bit labor intensive up front, the closer we inched toward Christmas, the fewer responsibilities we had. The team was asked to record a song for the churches in the local conference — about forty or so — who would view the service the Sunday after Christmas. It meant that since our contribution to that worship service was due a few weeks prior to Christmas, we had no worship commitments in the week following the holiday.

In a normal year, I stand up front with the worship team for much of the Christmas Eve worship service, which leaves my husband alone in a chair most of the night. I also arrive a few hours early to set up instruments and rehearse with the band, which further encroaches on any relaxing time at home the night before Christmas. The season often flows with frenzy amid the festivities.

Not last year. When Christmas Eve rolled around, my husband and I enjoyed the service together. We grabbed a laptop, positioned ourselves in front of the fireplace, and settled in for a peaceful evening. Once the worship service concluded, we closed the computer and read by the Christmas tree, holiday music playing softly in the background. No commute, no packing up instruments.

All was calm last Christmas Eve.

4

Christmas on the Go

Jean Matthew Hall

Over the river and through the woods,
　　Grandma's the one on the go.
In her Chevrolet she can't lose her way
　　with her new GPS in tow.

I-85 is easy to drive
　　in rain, in sleet, or in snow.
Holiday MP3s keep her company
　　when traffic is moving too slow.

Her trunk's fully packed by Radio Shack
　　with gadgets and gigas galore.
No time to bake pies. Can't miss jazzercize.
　　Bet she bought everything in the store.

5

The Miracle of the Christmas Rabbit

Constance Gilbert

As I trim the Christmas tree, I am reminded of the story attached to each ornament. The Plaster of Paris and beaded felt ornaments I made for our first Christmas together. The baking soda ones I made the next year. The unique, misshapen ones handmade by my son each year at school. Others represent our vacations, and the musicals I directed.

Before I hang this clown, let me tell you its story.

As the Children's Choir Director, I chose the Christmas musical for both my choir and the Sunday School children. Each year I looked for a fresh approach to the Christmas story so the children would enjoy, learn, and not get bored by the time we presented it. Reaching the hearts of the parents and guests was an additional challenge.

In 1981 I chose the Christmas musical fantasy, *Super Gift from Heaven* by Betty Hager and Fred Block.

The story takes place in a toy store. At midnight the dolls, clowns, stuffed animals, and other toys come to life. They are worried about what happens when they are sold and what people mean when they call them *gifts*.

The main character is an Easter rabbit that was never sold.

Her role was played by a teenage girl, who wore a gray rabbit costume.

As the story progresses, the antique dolls from the crèche explain the meaning of Jesus's birth. The dolls, animals, and toys learn that gifts are not just things, but also actions. This leads them to sew up the Easter bunny's torn seam and replace her vest with a red and green one for Christmas.

Rehearsals went well and the Sunday arrived to present our musical gift. The costumes were on and the props ready. Moms added the finishing touches: rosy cheeks, whiskers, and powered noses. Dolls, stuffed animals, toy soldiers, and clowns lined up for small drinks and last minute bathroom visits. As the excitement and anxiety increased so did the noise level. Soon we would pray and head upstairs.

The sanctuary was nearly full. But the rabbit, along with her costume, was missing!

After a few frantic phone calls, we learned our teen was with her father. And even though he had known for weeks about the musical, he would not let her leave for "church stuff."

I found our pastor and asked him, without an explanation, to start the service with a few Christmas carols. He agreed. Then I looked for a certain gray-haired lady, took her to the foyer and asked her to gather a few prayer warriors. I needed heavy-duty spiritual guidance to pull this musical off with no rabbit.

They gathered and began to pray, and I went to the pastor's office to figure how to salvage the night without disappointing the children or the audience. As I prayed and skimmed the script, I heard the carols. I peeked into the sanctuary. It was full of moms and dads, grandparents and guests, all eager to see their young ones. A few latecomers were seated in the foyer.

I went downstairs to quiet and line up the children for their entrance while I continued to pray for inspiration. I was deep in thought when the back door slammed.

There was our missing teen! She dashed in with her rabbit suit flying behind her. The children and my helpers cheered as a mom rushed to get the makeup for some whiskers.

"Tell me later what happened," I called after her.

Humming "Oh, what joy, we're gifts!" from the musical, I started the children down the aisles. The congregation was unaware that a crisis had been avoided. However, the prayer warriors smiled as our rabbit, with her long floppy ears, skipped on cue down the center aisle.

By the close of the musical, the toys and dolls realize they could only be a gift to one child or family, but what makes Jesus the Super Gift, is that He is a gift to everyone. We can *all* receive the Super Gift from Heaven.

For me, the greatest gift that night was the sparkle in the children's eyes and the tears throughout the audience. As the children filed out, I watched them receive well-deserved hugs and kisses, and encouraging words from their families. "Oh, what joy, we're gifts" in action.

Once everyone was headed home, our teenage Easter-bunny-turned-Christmas-rabbit, told me what had happened. Her father had berated her all day because of "this church stuff you've gotten into," and became verbally abusive after my phone call. In the midst of his screaming at her, he suddenly threw her the car keys and yelled, "Go!"

She ran before he changed his mind.

I told her about the prayer warriors. They had not prayed for guidance for me, as I had requested. Instead, they asked the Lord to touch her father's heart.

God did. I doubt her father ever knew he had given us a gift that night — our rabbit and evidence of a miracle!

Each year, as I hang this clown ornament on the tree, I remember my son was a clown in *Super Gift From Heaven,* which will always be known to me as *The Miracle of the Christmas Rabbit.* A small miracle compared to the birth of Christ, yet God still is in the miracle-business.

6

Anytime Gifts

Melissa Henderson

C hristmas 2020 was definitely different in many ways. Family gatherings had to be postponed or canceled. Church services to celebrate the birth of Jesus were held online. A few churches had a "reservation" system in place for those who wanted to attend worship services in person. Some Christmas parties and get-togethers were held following strict guidelines. Masks, social distancing, temperature checks, and no hugs were the protocol in many situations. Life held new ways of daily living.

Our family lives in different areas of the country. From Virginia to North Carolina to South Carolina and Texas, we have varying schedules and commitments. As Christmas 2020 drew closer, conversations began as to how we could possibly be together.

Vaccines were not yet available. Medical professionals recommended masks and social distancing as the best weapons to use against the spread of the coronavirus. Everyone in our family wanted to be safe and agreed to follow the guidelines.

We purchased Christmas presents, wrapped them, and placed them in a closet, in hopes of seeing our loved ones soon. Meanwhile we waited for the safe opportunity to gather together.

We wrote special notes in cards, then stamped, addressed and mailed those cards knowing the heartfelt messages were the closest we would get to some of the family until the vaccines were given or the virus was gone.

A small gathering of three to five people worked for some occasions. We missed the sounds and laughter of the entire family being together, yet we were happy to have the opportunity to share Christmas with some of the family.

I checked the wrapped presents in the closet daily, eventually noticing a bit of dust gathering on top of the packages. A soft cloth helped wipe away the dust particles, but tears moistened my eyes every time I opened the closet door and saw those gifts. They were a reminder of the change in the world and our daily life.

In April 2021 the beauifully wrapped Christmas presents continued to sit in the closet waiting to be shared with loved ones. Family discussions about receiving the vaccine and when everyone would feel comfortable traveling safely were a daily reminder of what had been and what we hoped for the future.

I was reminded that celebrating the birth of Christ doesn't have to happen only one day of the year. We have the opportunity to celebrate Christ in every moment of every day.

The Christmas gifts would be opened at some point. But Christ's gift — His message and His sacrifice — is forever. We can share His love at any time.

Anytime gifts are the best. Whether we are celebrating a special occassion or giving a gift because we want to show someone they are loved, an anytime gift can bring comfort and peace as we grow closer to God.

7

What Christmas Is to Me

Joy S. Taylor

The tree lights chase the shadows and glint off the hanging ornaments. The kids run to see it, like those who ran to be at Jesus's knee. The world, changing their focus, keeps them looking down at the carefully wrapped gifts beneath the tree.

Imagine yourselves seated around the tree. Take a break, move back some, and focus your gaze upward with me.

Look at the sparkle of the lights and the glint from the tinsel and ornaments, especially those representing special family memories or family no longer with you. Sigh for what they mean to you and look further up to notice how the gleam tries to imitate God's light bouncing across the crystal sea of His heavenly home. Move your glance higher and widen its field until you see how the shape of the tree points to the brilliant star at its top, representing the star that led the wise men to where Baby Jesus was. Recognize that the tree and its star direct us to Jesus.

Christmas is about the One born among the lambs in the stable; the Lamb to take away the sins of you and me on this broken earth. Jesus touched and blessed the children at His knee, and He touches and blesses us.

Again Jesus spoke to them, saying, "I am the light of the world. Whoever follows me will not walk in darkness, but will have the light of life." (John 8:12 ESV)

Listen to the children singing, and let the lyrics open a tender place in your heart as they whisper, "Jesus lives."

The carolers sing, "Star of wonder, star of night, star with royal beauty bright, westward leading, still proceeding, guide us to thy perfect light." Can you hear the message ring? "Yet, in thy dark streets shineth the everlasting light. The hopes and fears of all the years are met in thee tonight." They croon our loving lullaby, "Holy Infant, so tender and mild, sleep in heavenly peace. Sleep in heavenly peace."

Have you heard the Christmas bells chiming their song, revealing the mystery of the birth of Jesus? Have you experienced the shiver from the moving of the Holy Spirit at the thought of our true Messiah? Have you pondered the name, Emmanuel, and that it actually means *He is God with us*? Have you thought about your kindred relationship with this King of kings in the form of a babe? This infant, who came into this world humbly, rode into Jerusalem on a lowly donkey, and dragged the cross to Golgotha's height only days later, comes again as King of kings and Lord of lords.

Have you pondered, as Mary did, these things in your heart? Have you made the connection between Baby Jesus and your Almighty Lord, between your soul and your Savior? Does your spirit quicken as the time for His coming draws closer? Do you wait in anticipation of seeing Him face to face? First John 3:2 (ESV) tells us, *"Beloved, we are God's children now, and what we will be has not yet appeared; but we know that when he appears we shall be like him, because we shall see him as he is."*

I can't totally wrap my mind around all God plans and continues to do. I just know that my spirit bears witness with the Holy Spirit of His Truth. Try though I might not to believe, I find I cannot refute the truth He speaks in my heart and in my life. I am grateful He sent this infant, warrior, king and savior to call me to His side, giving me the right to call God, Abba Daddy. May Christmas be only about the Christ and His entrance to this side of nothing to bring us into something wonderful, something holy. May you experience God's loving touch and feel the warmth of His powerful arm across your shoulders. May you respond to the pull of the Holy Spirit drawing you to Jesus. May you see and know Jesus for who He really is. My prayer for you is that the hopes and fears of all your years are met in Jesus today.

8

Christmas Scavenger Hunt

Donna Collins Tinsley

What could celebrating Christmas and going on a scavenger hunt have in common? One year when my grandchildren were young, they both spoke of the "Spirit of Giving" to my family.

Every year I try to have an annual Christmas sleepover for my grandchildren. It is before Christmas of course, because they want to be at home on Christmas Eve. But their parents get a night to themselves to shop, or do whatever needed to be done before Christmas Day.

Now, the kids seem to prefer pizza and wings at their sleepover. How things have changed over the years! The tradition had been for me to cook a big family dinner for both grandkids and their parents. I always tried to offer several options to make sure it was a day when everyone could come, but the year Jordan ended up in the Emergency Room because he decided to swallow a coin put an end to that. His mom dropped him and his brother off after spending the day at the hospital. We were felt blessed that year just to have all the grandkids together.

When the grandkids were young the money I had for gifts seemed to go pretty far and it really looked like a Christmas morning as they opened numerous gifts. The older grandchildren knew the younger one's gifts were less expensive so they didn't mind that they might have fewer to open themselves. But one particular year when work for my husband's business nearly caved in with the economy, I was wondering how I was going make our Christmas sleepover a special blessing.

Although they were happy just to be together, because their ages ranged from fourteen months to fifteen years, entertaining them afterwards or the next day seemed to be the big question.

When I asked the kids about what they wanted to do, no one could agree on anything.

"Let's go play ball!" said Isaiah and Jordan.

"Let's watch *The Sandlot* instead!"

"Maybe we should sleep in," said Aubrey.

"Yeah, and then you could make pancakes and bacon and then Aubrey and I will make a peach dump cake and homemade caramels!" Austin's sweet tooth was aching to be satisfied.

"How can you even want anything else after all the chocolate covered pretzels and "Death by Chocolate" we had tonight?" I asked.

"Oh MeMa! It's Christmas!"

"That's true but it seems to me that we need to have more of the Christmas spirit around this house!" was my reply.

Deep in my heart I was afraid that Christmas was becoming more about presents than the *presence* of the Holy Season. It was making me sad until I remembered something we had done one year for one of my daughter's birthday party. We'd had a food scavenger hunt around the neighborhood and gave the food to a local food bank. We could do the same thing now.

I still had bags that were printed with a list of things like macaroni, canned vegetables, canned fruits, soups, and rice. These food items and more are all needed for those struggling within our community. People would know by looking at the bags and seeing the phone number they could call that ours was a legitimate cause.

We got the wagon out and started down the block. It was a brisk, sunny day in central Florida and I was walking with Aubrey, Austin, Jordan, little Isaiah, and toddler Aryel in the stroller. At first we found, with the economy the way it was and my grandchildren looking like a motley crew after staying up talking and playing all night long, many people were skeptical. After the children gave a little invitation to contribute, I made sure that people knew that even giving one can was just fine. When we all pull together it makes a big difference and food banks were really hurting those days. A few people declined giving but they were definitely in the minority. The kids had fun just walking around the neighborhood pulling the wagon of donations, with me pushing Aryel. And I could literally feel the Christmas Spirit of giving return to our family.

I had been in such a rush to get us out of the house and onto our mission that I hadn't noticed my five-year-old grandson, Isaiah, looked like a vagabond. He had remnants of hot chocolate on his face and we had forgotten to comb his hair in the excitement. He resembled something out of a Dickens story when he dashed ahead of the older children and ran to a door holding out his bag, saying, "Could I please have some food?" With his sweet freckles and bright red hair, who could refuse? (But I hurried up to the door to explain that he wasn't a starving little urchin but he just wanted to help some kids that might be in need.)

Although at first it looked like we wouldn't have much to donate, we ended up having enough food to take some to the Domestic Abuse Thrift Store also. The teenagers had bowed out by that time, but the pictures I took of the little ones in front of the ministry will always be a special reminder of our new Christmas tradition.

Do you want a Christmas blessing? Try a Christmas scavenger hunt! Any scavenger hunt is fun, but I think that Christmas scavenger hunt might have been the best one yet!

9

The Cookie Bake

Elberta Clinton
as told to Helen L. Hoover

Making homemade cookies close to Christmas is a life-long occurrence for me. I have wonderful memories of cookie baking from over a seventy-five-year period — first with my mother, next with our three daughters, then our six granddaughters, and with a friend. It is a Christmas tradition that I dearly love.

I remember — as a preschooler — my mother helping me roll out sugar cookie dough on the surface of an old white-enamel kitchen safe. "I want to make heart-shaped ones," I told her. It was fun to use the special shaped cookie cutters an aunt had sent. I sprinkled colored sugar on the cookies and then licked my fingers.

Those cutters have been used repeatedly over the years by myself and my family.

After cleaning up the kitchen, mother and I put an assortment of freshly-baked cookies in a basket and took them to a neighbor family. "Oh look, there is a blue angel!" one child exclaimed. "I like the green tree," another child said. "Thank you! Thank you!" the children repeated to us as they gave us hugs.

The years of baking cookies with my mother quickly passed.

As my husband's and my three daughters grew old enough to watch and then help, the Saturday a couple of weeks before Christmas became the day for making holiday cookies.

"I want to make a yellow star for my teacher. She tells us about the stars in the heavens," ten-year-old Lynn said. "I'll make a pink angel for my friend Suzie. She is so nice to everyone," nine-year-old Kim announced. "Mommy, Mommy, help me make a red heart for Daddy," three-year-old Sandy pleaded.

After a day of making cookies, the house smelled wonderful as the five of us gorged on the delicious, warm cookies. We always had enough to give to the neighbors, the girls' schoolteachers, and family friends.

Soon our daughters grew up, married, and provided us with granddaughters who love to bake Christmas cookies, too. The younger girls talk about the coming event for days before the bake day. "What cookies will we make? Will we have enough to take to school and share with friends?"

Three of our granddaughters are now college age, one is in high school, and two are in elementary school. It thrills this grandma's heart that they still want to come for the cookie bake. They comment on the variety of cookies we have made in the past, who they were given to, and who got the most flour on her clothing.

We have made a variety of cookies over the years, including the rolled-out sugar cookies, chocolate chip cookies, snickerdoodles, Russian tea cakes, gingerbread men, and cranberry white chocolate oatmeal.

One year, a young mother from church came to my house for a cookie bake. We made sixty gingerbread men for our church Christmas coffee. Each lady there received a cookie with the icing and candies to decorate the cookie as they desired. "This is so much fun, I haven't decorated cookies for many, many years" one delighted senior said. The women considered it a great treat. It was a treat for the young mother and me, too.

The 2020 pandemic put a stop to various family traditions, but I decided to just change the cookie baking a little so we could continue with our cookie memories. I made five homemade cookie kits that included huge prebaked gingerbread men, icing, and decorating candies. I hoped this substitute for our regular cookie bake would be special.

One of these kits went to each daughter's family, one to a single friend, and one to the young mother who had helped me several years earlier. The idea met with enthusiasm from all the recipients and brought another dimension to our annual event.

I am pleased to see cookie baking continue with my family. My two youngest daughters participate in Christmas cookie exchanges in their own neighborhoods. Granddaughter Chloe, now eighteen, bakes fresh cookies for her family all during the year. She treasures the one-handle rolling pin and the vintage gingerbread man cookie cutter that once were her great-grandmother's.

It was especially endearing a few years ago when I asked two teenage granddaughters if they wanted to continue with the cookie baking. "Why would you think we didn't want to?" the oldest granddaughter asked.

I don't know what another Christmas will bring, but hopefully it will still include a cookie bake in some form.

10

Christmas Expectations

Jeanetta Chrystie

What was I expecting?
Holidays of cheer,
Days filled with busy-ness
As Christmas-time drew near.

No holiday or human
Can satisfy my soul.
I shove my expectations deep
Like hands on a winter's stroll.

When did I learn to put my hopes
On long-term layaway,
Like packages for Christmas
That I'll redeem someday?

Oh, come thou long-expected Jesus.
Set my spirit free.
Bring Christmas to my heart today.
Let me exult in Thee.

Were You Born in a Barn?

Diana C. Derringer

She gave birth to her firstborn, a son.
She wrapped him in cloths and placed him in a manger,
because there was no guest room available for them.

Luke 2:7 NIV

Like many children, my sister and I were better at opening than closing. Cabinet doors swung over the counter. Jars of peanut butter sat without their lids. Dresser drawers drooped with clothes spilling out.

The negligent habit that irritated our mother most was our leaving the front or back door open. In the winter, heat escaped. In the summer, heat and flies rushed in. Each time we failed to shut one completely, Mom's voice rang out, "Close the door! Were you born in a barn?"

No, we weren't. In fact, we experienced the luxury of a modern hospital. Doctors and nurses assisted in our delivery. They wrapped us snugly in diapers, booties, and blankets. Friends and family oohed and aahed at our cuteness.

We often take all those benefits — and more —for granted.

I know someone who *was* born in a barn. However that looked — whether a cave, a separate stable, or an attachment to a house — Jesus was born in a shelter for animals and placed in a feeding trough. He had no hospital, no doctors or nurses, no friends or extended family nearby. Instead of in a blanket, He was wrapped in strips of cloth.

When we open the door of our lives to Jesus, His gift of love and forgiveness rushes in, forcing out the curse of sin and death.

At Christmas and always, I thank God for the peace of divine presence made possible through the gift of Jesus's birth.

An Outsider's Christmas

Marv Stone

I've always been an outsider in my wife's family. We've lived in this very small town in north Mississippi for twenty-five years, but seeing how I was born in Alabama, I'm considered to be "not from around here." The fact that I'm a die-hard Alabama fan doesn't help my case for citizenship either. But I do believe all of that could be forgiven if not for my most grievous fault . . . I don't like Bird. Don't get me wrong, I have nothing against birds. I actually like them. I have feeders all around my home and even help keep the ones at the local nursing home filled. There is nothing more depressing than an empty bird feeder. So, it's not birds that are the problem. It's Bird.

Every Christmas Eve, Mary Dean's family all gather at my sister-in-law's home for the traditional Eating of The Quail. The ritual started two generations back with my wife's grandparents. At that time, the event was a culmination of a big family hunt-clean-and-cook Christmas project. Today they buy the quail but still keep to the clean-and-cook portion of the tradition. If not for war stories about the effort involved in cleaning "the bird," we'd only have "the game" to talk about around the dinner table.

Apparently, every quail has a wishbone that is carefully preserved during the consumption of said bird. Afterwards, two family members pull on each side of the bone, and the one left with the short end is declared the winner of "the game." These contests are taken quite seriously, and even though no prize is awarded, bragging and taunting follow each win. My sister-in-law almost always beats my wife, but then again, according to my wife, she cheats.

This brings us to the primary cause of my outsider status with Mary Dean's family. The first few years we were married, I would partake of The Christmas Bird and make all the appropriate comments regarding how good it tasted and that I was sure it was better than the year before. But when my son was born, setting an example of honesty in my life became more important. I could no longer lie to everyone concerning the quail.

The Christmas I made this declaration of culinary honesty sealed my fate. I had already upset the apple cart the year before by announcing that Santa Claus would be coming to our house instead of the grandparents' home in Columbus, thus ending one enduring Christmas tradition. This, coupled with the confession that I didn't like The Christmas Bird, made me the family Grinch.

Every Christmas since, my brother-in-law has made a big show of cooking me chicken strips along with the quail in his fryer. I feel like I'm eating off the kid's menu, but at least I still get to sit at the adults' table.

This brings us to the Christmas of 2020, the Covid Christmas. My sister-in-law, who hosts the annual Eating of the Quail, has two daughters. One of them works in public relations for a local hospital, and the other is a pharmacist. So, both had a bird's-eye view, pardon the pun, to the crisis caused by the pandemic. Because of their concerns, which were wholly justified, we'd had ongoing negotiations around the Eating of the Quail event for months. Finally, a week before the big night, an agreement acceptable to all parties was reached.

It was then that my son Billy, now twenty-three and very respectful of my example of living an honest life, disclosed that his girlfriend and all her family had tested positive for "the virus," as it was known in our circle.

Now, he had no symptoms, but having been twenty-three and in love once myself, I was fairly certain that he and his girlfriend had not been observant of social distancing. So, the week before Christmas, my family and I entered quarantine for the first time. You can imagine the weeping and moaning and gnashing of teeth that permeated our home.

I must admit, however, in the spirit of my honest life, I was kind of looking forward to a Christmas without the taunts of "Chicken Boy" being thrown around the table.

The three of us, my wife, my son, and I, settled on a Christmas Eve meal sans bird and sent my sister-in-law to the store with our list. She offered to bring some bird to our home that evening, but being the loving brother-in-law I am, I did not want her to have to leave her family, so I declined. We had steaks off the grill instead, something I once only imagined in my wildest holiday fantasies!

Christmas morning, normally full of haste and fury as everyone gathers at our house for brunch and presents, was quiet and peaceful. I got up when I woke up, not in a hurry to start cooking and preparing, and sat with Annabelle, our dog, while enjoying a wonderful cup of coffee. Mary Dean joined me later and finally, Billy. We leisurely ate our pancakes and then exchanged presents. We watched *It's a Wonderful Life* twice and did a whole lot of nothing the rest of the day.

All in all, a great Christmas.

Now, don't get me wrong, I love our entire family being together during the holidays. A "normal" season starts with a huge Thanksgiving dinner. Then we have movie night at our house where we watch the Christmas movie selected by online voting — yes, I run the voting, and we have had occasional calls for election reform! — and we eat chili. Christmas Eve together at church is followed by the earlier-described culminating events. So, I did miss the togetherness and fellowship of Christmas Eve and morning, but as my son so eloquently stated: "Christmas with just us. I'm down with that!"

As planning for The Eating of the Quail 2021 swings into full gear this year, I can't help but nostalgically look back on 2020. I do understand the negative impact the pandemic has had on so many folks, but our own quarantine was a kind of Christmas reprieve. We enjoyed the season, the food, and each other more than we have in many years. Therefore, I've made a resolution to myself this year. As the wishbone battles are fought and the "Chicken Boy" cries ring out, I will keep Christmas in my heart the whole night through, remembering family and friends and reflecting that God has indeed already blessed us, every one.

13

A Country-School Christmas

Beverly Robertson

It's been a long time since anyone experienced a one-room country school with nine grades. Have you? If not, just imagine how busy our teacher was with so much going on. Then imagine how much busier she must have been at Christmastime.

As elementary students in the early 1950's, we excitedly welcomed Christmas. Preparation began several weeks ahead of time. We made garlands for a tree by fashioning multi-colored paper chains out of construction paper. Then we strung popcorn together. (Some disappeared in the process.) Snowflakes were cut from white paper as we attempted to create different designs. The younger children had help from our teacher.

When someone donated a large fir tree, which to our eyes seemed mammoth, we proudly put everything on it with the taller kids reaching for the top.

And of course, there was a Christmas program. We performed in front of our parents, grandparents, and other family members, but were as nervous as if we were in front of a Broadway audience.

The teacher handed out poems and sayings for younger pupils to memorize. The program always ended with a play in which the older students were given parts. We practiced those parts for days.

To create our stage, a wire was strung from wall to wall and sheets were hung and fastened with large safety pins so as to slide along the line. Two children were chosen to open and close the makeshift drapes, which made a screeching sound when pulled back and forth.

The anticipated day of the performance came and everyone in the community looked forward to the big event. Desks and chairs were filled with family members and friends waiting expectantly while feet scurried behind the curtains.

The littlest performers were loved regardless of whether they forgot their lines or waved to the audience. Older students were able to show off their singing or acting abilities.

After the play, everyone sang Christmas carols. Then the big event happened.

Sleigh bells rang from somewhere outside the back of the building and the door opened. The jingling continued down the middle aisle of the room. Excited younger siblings stood on their parents' chairs and laughed as Santa made his big entrance.

From his huge bag, Santa pulled out a little box for each child. We eagerly looked inside to find mostly hard candy, but we were delighted to also discover two or three chocolate drops. It was a special treat to have our own stash of candy.

The evening closed with cookies and punch.

Down through the years, Christmas at our one-room country school stands out as one of my treasured memories.

14

The Letterman's Jacket

Jennifer A. Doss

My senior year in high school brought about a lot of growth for me. I'd finally been brave enough to try out and become part of the cheerleading squad. I wasn't any good but I was strong and stout and made a good base for pyramids or stunts.

I'd always been in choir, but the day they handed me my choir letter for my letterman's jacket, I was in love. The stitches created a beautiful design and the sturdy backing was made to be attached to a heavy jacket. I knew I would get a varsity cheer letter too.

From that moment, I begged my parents for a letterman's jacket. We couldn't afford it; that was no secret. But it didn't stop my persistence.

* * *

"What do you want for Christmas?" Mother asked. It was how she ensured we all got things we wanted and would use. Every September or October, she would have us make a list so she could gradually buy gifts as they could afford them.

"My letterman's jacket," came my instant reply.

"Honey, you know we can't afford that."

I knew. Very well. I don't think my parents spent that kind of money on the four of us kids combined. Even though gifts for my siblings who were seven, nine, and eleven were less expensive and easier, my parents wouldn't spend more on one child than another. That wasn't how they did things. My mother tried to spend the exact same amount on each of us. If she found something on sale, she'd use the savings to buy another small item.

I stalked away. In my one-track mind, nothing else mattered. I honestly couldn't come up with a single other item I wanted.

"What do you want for Christmas?" she asked me weeks later.

"My letterman's jacket," I replied again.

She shook her head and walked away. "If you don't give me some ideas, I'll just have to buy you random things or maybe nothing," she warned.

Every time the subject came up my reply was the same. My parents became increasingly frustrated. Maybe they wouldn't get me anything then. Did it matter if there were no gifts under the tree for me?

I considered it. Yes, it did. I would be sad and disappointed without gifts, but there was only one thing I wanted under the tree.

"I picked out some gifts for you," Mother said on Christmas Eve. "I hope you like them."

"Mmmhmmm," I mumbled. Gifts? If there was more than one, it couldn't be the jacket. *Stop it!* I chastised myself. *You're acting like a spoiled brat.*

"I'm sure I'll love what you got me," I said aloud. If my attitude didn't change I was going to ruin the holiday for all of us. I'd just have to save money from my job to get the jacket. I still had time, I just wouldn't get to wear the jacket to school. The thought saddened me but at least I had a plan.

On Christmas morning, we gathered around the tree, Dad handing gifts out one by one and announcing who each was from. My brothers and sister got gift after gift. A doll, some books, new clothes, Legos. Not a single gift came my way. Maybe my mother really didn't get me anything. It was my own fault if that was the case.

I wished I had given her a list. I could've come up with some things so I wasn't sitting there with nothing to open. I hated my selfishness and exaggerated my excitement over my siblings' gifts.

When all the presents appeared to have been handed out Dad said,

"Oh, Jennifer, here's one for you."

He handed me a large rectangular box.

It wasn't. It couldn't be. But it was the right size and shape. If this was a trick. . . .

I peeled the paper off carefully, afraid of what might be inside. As I lifted the lid, a perfect green and white letterman's jacket with "Jennifer" embroidered across the back lay inside. My eyes filled with tears.

"How did you? You got my jacket?" I blubbered out the words in disbelief. They couldn't afford it. There was no way. Where could they have gotten the money? Only it didn't matter. Both of my parents glowed at my reaction. They were so proud to be able to give me the jacket, and I was ecstatic as I slid my arms into the sleeves and paraded around.

I wore that jacket every day for months, even when it got too warm outside for jackets. It was special, a sacrifice. And still today, almost thirty years later, it hangs in my closet, a precious memento that reminds me of sacrificial love. I don't know what they gave up to get that gift for me, but I know it was worth much more than the money they paid.

15

God Revealed the True Meaning of Christmas

Diana Leagh Matthews

I t's the Most Wonderful Time of the Year." Yes, as the song says, Christmas is a wonderful time of year. I love the spirit of the season, but most importantly that we celebrate the birth of Jesus Christ. Without Christmas we cannot have Easter.

However, Christmas is also my busiest time of the year. Each year, from Halloween to Epiphany, the season flies by in a whirlwind of activity. To be honest I get overwhelmed at times.

As the activity director for a busy rehabilitation center and skilled nursing home, it is my responsibility to oversee all the decorating and festivities. It is not limited to only Christmastime. Throughout the year, I am responsible for raising funds for the residents' Christmas presents. By August, the work of planning has begun to schedule the various groups who will assist with our needs and create a timeline which is not too stressful and overwhelming. Over the years, I had perfected this schedule and knew the groups on which I could depend.

Then Covid happened and it became clear Christmas 2020 would be different. For months, I stressed over how to make Christmas special for our residents and where the money would come from to pull off such an endeavor. With the residents unable to see their family members,

I longed to make the holiday even more special for them. And so, I began to pray and ask the Lord for guidance and wisdom.

With the facility on lockdown, there were a handful of months we were unable to hold our monthly Blue Plate Special or any other fundraising endeavors. In September, letters went out to the various groups who assisted us, asking for help. The lack of response disappointed me.

However, the Lord showed up and blessed our residents through many people I never expected.

Over the years, I had resisted a Christmas Angel Tree for fear the staff would not participate. However, the staff response blew me away and within three days all sixty-five of our long-term residents had a staff "angel." Christmas presents soon poured in, overflowing the offices. Staff were asked to place presents in a gift bag, which eliminated the need to wrap all of them.

Several staff members stepped up and assisted my team and I with decorating. We downsized our decorations and put up eight trees instead of the usual twenty-three our youth volunteers helped set up.

Then a carload of supplies arrived, items for Christmas stockings, donated by another volunteer. My heart overflowed with gratitude as my team and I prepared the stockings.

Even my writing friends got in on the action, sending in monetary donations and boxes of tissues for all the residents. And blankets were donated for all our short-term rehab patients.

In lieu of Santa's Workshop, which we hold every year for the residents to purchase a gift for their family, we arranged for a Christmas drive-up. This allowed families to drive up in their cars and see their loved ones for a short visit. During this time, they were able to talk, exchange gifts, and blow kisses from afar. Instead of residents purchasing presents for their loved ones, my staff and I took a picture of the resident, as well as a picture of their hands. I had seen many comments online about how much family members appreciated having a picture of their loved one's hands, especially after they passed. We framed and wrapped both pictures for the resident to give to their family. The tears in the eyes of these loved ones as they opened their presents filled my heart with happiness. For days afterward, I received calls of thanks.

On the day of our Christmas party, two different church groups unexpectedly dropped off Christmas stockings for our residents. My heart soared at the kindness bestowed on us.

To prolong the celebration, we counted down the twelve days leading to Christmas. Each day, we discussed the significance of the holiday and hung an ornament for that day on the Christmas tree in the activity room. We also read a traditional Christmas story daily, ending with the best story of all on Christmas Day. The story found in Luke 2.

We asked our residents how they would like to celebrate during their Christmas party, since we were unable to have outside entertainment. They voted on a sing-along of Christmas songs and carols and had a wonderful time.

Earlier in the week, our staff dressed up as "The Grinch Who Stole Christmas" which the residents also loved. Although the Grinch tried to steal Christmas, we would not let him snatch the joy of the season.

The week of Christmas we held a birthday party for the Christ child and studied the true meaning of Christmas during Bible Study.

While I had no idea how things would come together for Christmas 2020 or how to make it special for my residents, I turned to the Lord. After all, Jesus said, "*Ask, and it will be given to you; seek, and you will find; knock, and it will be opened to you.*" (Matthew 7:7 ESV)

My heart broke when I heard from other activity directors who were unable to do anything for their residents. From my first year on the job, I'd resolved to do everything possible to make Christmas special. No matter what it took.

This year, it took leaning on my faith as never before.

I asked and the Lord provided in unique and unexpected ways.

As for me, I learned to trust the Lord and get out of my own way so He could work. Jesus reminds us, "*Look at the birds of the air: they neither sow nor reap nor gather into barns, and yet your heavenly Father feeds them. Are you not of more value than they? And which of you by being anxious can add a single hour to his span of life?"* (Matthew 6:26-27, ESV)

Jesus went above and beyond in providing for our residents and making Christmas 2020 special for them.

It is a Christmas none of us will forget.

How has God shown up and provided in your life? What is an event you'll never forget?

16

God With Us

Terri R. Miller

The Christmas of 2017 went much the same as every other Christmas has gone for my family since my brother and I have been grown with families of our own. We gathered at my parents' house for a day of food, gifts, playing games and just being together. Now that all our children are grown, it has taken a Herculean effort to coordinate everyone's schedule and find one day that works, but we had somehow managed it.

The menu didn't vary much from previous years. There was the usual oven-roasted turkey breast, Mama's cornbread dressing and gravy, and green beans. Delaine, my sister-in-law, brought her cherry salad, and I contributed the sweet potato casserole. All of this and more lined the counter by the stove. As usual the opposite counter, designated as the dessert counter, held a truly shameful number of cakes, pies, cookies, and candies.

Over the years, my parents' Christmas tree had gone from a handpicked wonderfully aromatic live tree to an artificial tree. Now, even that was reduced from its original full size to just a four-foot mini tree perched on top of the sewing machine cabinet. Twinkling multi-colored lights adorned its branches, and gifts littered the floor below all ready for a game of Dirty Santa.

We enjoyed our food as we discussed topics ranging from politics to trips down memory lane. Lingering there at the table enjoying everyone's company has always been one of my favorite parts of the day. Once the meal was over and the kitchen put back in order, we each took a place in the living room ready for the game and the unwrapping of gifts. But first, Mama asked for a volunteer to read the Christmas story. Although this had been done sporadically when my brother and I were growing up, some time back my mom and dad made a conscious effort to have it as part of the family tradition when we are gathered around the tree before gifts are exchanged.

My daughter-in-law, Tori, offered to read. She sat on the floor, the Bible lying before her on the large ottoman and opened to Luke's account of the story. As she read, I thought of how fitting it was that she should be the one to read this year. Her rounded belly nestled my unborn grandson. A child. A son. A gift to us all.

It was a beautiful time together as a family — filled with laughter and love — and when it was over, we moved into the new year taking for granted that we would continue with the status quo indefinitely. There was no way we could have known as we spent that day together that we were perched on the edge of life as we knew it about to plunge headlong into uncharted waters. Nothing would ever be the same again.

A few short weeks later, in early January, my dad suffered a stroke. A brain bleed is what the doctor said. Thankfully he survived, but not without some limitations. He can walk on his own but is sometimes unsteady. The risk of falling is always present. Because he can no longer drive, the frequent long trips my parents had become accustomed to have come to an end. My dad was the principal driver and my mom isn't comfortable driving in unfamiliar places.

They own a large amount of property and need help taking care of that. We had some 'work' days where everyone came together and pitched in, but for the most part my brother and his wife took over things like mowing the grass, tending the garden, and general repairs and upkeep, because they live much closer than we do. My brother has gracefully stepped up and taken responsibility for many of the things that my dad would normally have done. I have been amazed as I've watched him walk out his new role with the utmost tenderness and respect for my dad.

Daddy's huge woodworking shop — always humming with the sounds of saws and lathes and where he built baby beds, blanket chests, and beehives — is now silent. Unfinished projects and piles of wood for projects dreamed of lie untouched.

You may be asking yourself what all of this has to do with Christmas. That Christmas, like every Christmas before it and every Christmas since, we celebrated the fact that the Eternal God who existed before the foundation of the world stepped into time becoming fully human. In one of the most humble settings imaginable, The King of kings came to us. Came *for* us. The Child who was born. The Son who was given. A gift to us all.

As I look back on that Christmas before Daddy's stroke, I can see Jesus there, seated at the table with us as we broke bread and shared ourselves with each other, gathered with us around the tree listening to the story of His birth. As we laughed and played games, the Light of the World was sealing our hearts together in love and the knowledge that He was the center of our family.

Jesus is with us now, too, as we learn to make our way on this new journey. Each time we must cross a bridge that we haven't crossed before, He's there giving us the grace to honor one another in the choices that we make, and stirring up compassion in our hearts for each other. Our time together now is richer and sweeter because we understand its value. He's helped us not to lose sight of that. Though we've always been an affectionate family, hugs now are tighter and the "I love you's" are more earnest.

Because Jesus is not bound by time, He has simultaneously been with us in the past, is with us now in the present, and has gone before us into the future preparing the way and beckoning us with outstretched hand to come and not be afraid. We don't know what lies ahead, but He has already been there making a path for us to follow. What a comforting thought to know that there is no place or time where we can go that He has not already gone.

At Christmastime, I'm reminded once again that the Lord of heaven and Earth wrapped Himself in flesh and walked among us. He was with us then. He is with us still. He is Emanuel, God with us.

17

The Three Trees

Sue Rice

They were the last trees left on the lot. Shorty, a Douglas Fir, got his name when a little boy had proclaimed him "just my size." Robin, an attractive Scotch Pine, got his name when a bird had tried to build a nest in his branches. And Kingston, the stately third remaining tree, was a tall, majestic Balsam Fir.

The leftover trees were no longer mounted in tree stands. The drugstore's owner had moved them and leaned them against the storefront so shoppers had to pass them going into the store.

"What if no one wants us?" Shorty asked. It was two o'clock in the morning. All the activity had stopped and the trees could finally talk about their dilemma. "It's getting very close to Christmas."

"It's not like they can't see how good looking I am," Kingston said.

"There's nothing wrong with any of us," Robin told the other two. "We have to trust that God has a plan for each of us."

The next day the three trees hoped in vain to catch the eye of the last-minute shoppers who hurried into the store. But it was so cold nobody was taking time to notice them.

"We're the best buy at this store," Kingston remarked as a woman dragged her young son away when he slowed to touch Shorty. Kingston was reaching for the sky, holding himself at attention. Robin was trying his best to lose a plastic bag that had flattened itself against his branches.

With just two days left till Christmas, the store manager placed a FREE sign on the three trees.

A young woman carrying several bags and a baby felt the pull of her five-year-old son as they passed. "Please Mommy. Can I have this tree? It's just my size."

She thought of how lucky they were that her son had survived his recent battle with cancer. "All right. Help me take it to the van."

Kingston felt a stab of envy as they lifted Shorty and took him away. Robin waved his branches at him, happy for Shorty's good fortune.

A little later Kingston noticed a van on the street about to pass him and Robin. It slowed to a stop and a man in a red jacket hopped out and approached them. He lifted Robin onto his shoulder, then walked quickly back to the van marked Peoples' Shelter.

Robin was going to be a Christmas tree at a shelter downtown! How exciting! Robin finally had an important assignment. He puffed out his branches, waved toward Kingston, and said a prayer that Kingston would soon find a home too.

But when nighttime came again Kingston was alone.

Christmas Eve dawned colder than the day before. The store opened shortly after sunrise and people were once again in a big hurry to get from their warm cars into the heated store and back.

Kingston said a silent prayer. "Please God, Robin said that everything you create has a purpose. I want so much to be a Christmas tree."

But soon the store was closing and employees were calling out Merry Christmas to one another as they left.

"It's over!" thought Kingston. "No one will ever open presents that have been placed at my feet. No star or angel will decorate my head. I'm just a big old nothing."

The moon peeked out from behind the clouds scurrying across the sky. It seemed to wink when Kingston looked upward to the heavens. A sudden whoosh of wind swept Kingston near the busy road.

"Oh no! Now I'll be nothing more than twigs and needles."

A passing car pulled over. The man who had been driving jumped out and grabbed Kingston.

"Look Marie!" he exclaimed. "You just prayed for a sign that God still loves us. We might not have money for presents but look at this handsome tree. Let's stop at your mother's house and see if she has some extra ornaments."

Kingston smiled. Robin had been right. God has a perfect plan for everyone and everything.

18

The Well of Christmas Despair

Lynn Mosher

Christmas 2020 is one that will not be soon forgotten. It was a time of rejoicing in the midst of a pandemic.

Was it off the norm or remarkable for you?

As for us . . . we missed our family gathering at my brother's house. And our first son and his fiancée didn't join us at our house. No granddaughters. To say ours was an unusual Christmas would be an understatement.

However, we were able to celebrate with our second son and his fiancée who moved in with us.

For many, though, that Christmas was a time of loneliness and a feeling of disconnect.

Some lacked finances for gifts; some lost jobs and homes. Some were separated from family due to travel restrictions, quarantine, or cautiousness.

Whatever the reason, for many, it felt like a well of despair.

The phrase *"well of despair"* reminds me of a line of dialog from an episode of the television wartime series M*A*S*H. It is about a situation of being separated from one's family at Christmas.

In this episode, Dr. Charles Emerson Winchester III, a.k.a. Snootyface, is depressed, "waxing nostalgic" as he calls it, and would much rather be at home in Boston with his family gathered around the fireplace, with all its "utter civility."

Unbeknownst to Charles, Radar, the company clerk, had written to Charles' mother at the suggestion of the chaplain, Father Mulcahy, asking that she send something that might make Charles feel more at home — even in his hostile surroundings — and bring him a little ray of hope.

Charles' mother sends an old toboggan cap from Charles' youth, and when he opens the package, he is totally delighted. With the small cap stretched over his bocce-ball head, Charles cleans out his pockets of all his cash and gives it to the chaplain for the local orphans.

Father Mulcahy, puzzled by Charles' sudden generosity, asks, "Major, are you all right?"

Chuckling and patting his capped head, Charles says, "You saved me, Father. You lowered a bucket into the well of my despair and you raised me up to the light of day. I thank you for that."

For many, Christmas presents any number of serious personal wars: depression, heartache, loneliness, frustration, relationship riffs, and other disheartening situations.

Maybe you have your own well of Christmas despair, your own personal war. Who reaches down into that well and lifts you up to the light of day?

Christ is always there to do so. Any one of us can dip into His well of hope and be refreshed.

Do you see others drinking from the well of despair during the Christmas season? Offer them a drink from the well of Living Water to give them hope.

Lift *them* up to see the light of day, to see Jesus as their Light.

This Christmas and every Christmas the Father is sending you hope and encouragement from home through the miracle of the manger — the birth of His Son, Jesus.

"And in His name all oppression shall cease.
Sweet hymns of joy in grateful chorus raise we,
With all our hearts we praise His holy name."

O holy night, O night divine!
O night divine, indeed!

May your Christmas be filled with overwhelming joy, no matter what your circumstances may be.

19

Cherry Chocolate Christmas

Diana L. Walters

Having an angel tree topper had been a family tradition my entire life. The one I place on the tree today isn't the original angel, but the story of how she came to be has become as much a family tradition as the angel herself.

Thirty years earlier I wasn't able to get into the holiday spirit. As Christmas approached, I felt an overwhelming sadness. For weeks, the kids had begged me to decorate the tree, but I had put it off until the week before Christmas. Finally, though, the lights were strung, ready for ornaments and tinsel.

"Well, let's get this show on the road." I sighed as I reached inside a huge plastic bin to withdraw smaller cardboard boxes.

Jennie held out her hands. "Let me put mine on first." I handed her a decorated shoebox full of felt ornaments my mother had made the previous year: Woodstock, Snoopy, Charlie Brown, and Lucy.

"Chris, you can put yours on the tree, too." My sixteen-year-old tore himself away from TV long enough to hang his cartoon characters.

When I pulled out a small, stocking-shaped piece of plywood, Jennie exclaimed, "Don't put that on the tree, it's ugly." It was the first ornament she'd decorated as a toddler. Mom had raved over her artistic talent.

I continued digging in the box, finding more ornaments Mom had made over the years: a bell made from crystal beads, a crocheted bear, and felt rocking horses. One horse was labeled "Jenny," the other "Kris" in gold glitter. Mom could never remember how to spell her grandchildren's names. By the time I was twelve years old, she had begun asking *me* how to spell words. "I don't need to be good at spelling when I have such a smart daughter," she'd laugh, her blue eyes dancing.

Mom had always been laughing.

Mom was good at other things besides spelling. She was good at making us laugh. And good at loving us unconditionally. She was good at cheerfully handling circumstances others would have cried over. Her mantra was, "God's in his heaven, all's right with the world."

Finally, all ornaments were hung. There was one small, wooden box left. It contained the remnants of the angel that had graced our tree throughout my childhood. Mom had given it to me to sit atop my first tree as a married woman. "I'm going to shop for a new angel," she'd said, "but you always loved this one, so I want you to have her for a keepsake." The angel wasn't in good shape even then, but I displayed her for several years before an arm came off and she became too fragile to hang. Now she resided in a box, wrapped in tissue paper. Her blond wig had come unglued and her broken arm lay next to her. The plastic dress was cracked in several places.

Mom never found a new angel. She settled for a star that glowed softly. My kids also opted for a star that twinkled red and green.

I didn't give up searching for replacement angels for Mom and me. Over the years I'd examined hundreds of angels, but I never found one I liked.

I quit searching in February when Mom passed away.

I'd attended a grief support group for a while, and it had helped, but as Christmas approached, I again felt overwhelming sadness. I made another appointment with Marti, the grief counselor. "I know Mom's in a better place, but I miss her and I'm beginning to forget the sound of her laughter. I feel like crying all the time."

Marti assured me it was natural to grieve again on my first Christmas without Mom. "This is a bump in the road, but it will get better." Then she added, "I'm going to give you an assignment."

I smiled. This was a familiar refrain from former sessions. Sometimes I was assigned to write down my feelings. Sometimes I was told to yell at an empty chair. I remembered pounding a pillow and crying like a five-year-old, "I want my mother."

Marti said, "Your assignment is to buy yourself a Christmas present. It will be from your mom. When you come back, we'll talk about what she got you."

I said okay, although it seemed like a silly exercise. After all, it wouldn't bring her back.

Mom had loved Christmas and would have had a pile of gifts waiting under the tree by now — some things she'd bought and others she'd made. She'd loved receiving presents as much as giving them. It didn't matter what it was. When she opened something, her glee was effusive, almost child-like. She emoted over the predictable box of cherry chocolates — something we gave her every year — as if it were a diamond necklace. "It's just what I wanted," she'd say. And she meant it.

I headed to Ben Franklin's to look for a present. After all, Mom wouldn't have bought something from an expensive gift shop. I wandered through the household goods and cruised past the jewelry counter. Nothing there. I drifted downstairs where toys and Christmas decorations were displayed. I strolled past lights, bulbs and tinsel, to a display of angels dressed in red, green, and gold dresses.

They were too gaudy.

I was turning away from the display when I glimpsed an angel in back of the others. This one wasn't quite like Mom's. Instead of a plastic dress, she wore white satin and had lace on her wings. A small beaded halo perched over her head. Instead of a silk wig, her blond hair was sculpted on. But the face! The face was what drew me to her; beautiful blue eyes, lips curved into a welcoming smile. So much like the face of the angel I'd grown up with.

I told the clerk "This is amazing! This is the angel I've been looking for all these years!"

"That's nice, dear."

"It's more than nice! It's an answer to prayer." It was like Mom really had sent me a gift — a gift from heaven.

Every year since, as the new angel looks down from our treetop, I feel Mom celebrating Christmas with us. God is in His heaven, all's right with the world. And Mom is with Him.

I imagine my mother smiling when she sees my grandchildren hand me the customary box of cherry chocolates.

I tell them it's just what I wanted.

20

Forever Christmas

Jane Owen

Celebrating Christmas for more than seven decades, my heart holds memories galore. But the one most memorable for me is Christmas 1950.

On Christmas Eve, I waited anxiously on the couch while listening to the sounds of shuffling paper and snipping scissors. I pictured my mother wrapping gifts in the next room and pondered her words of warning: "Janie, you must promise not to come into the dining room until I call you."

I'd agreed to stay put in the front room but wondered if I could sneak a peek around the corner. I folded my arms. *I can't break my promise. Santa would know for sure!*

Scooting to the floor, I focused on the stable scene nestled under the sparkling lights of our tree. Carefully, I wound the music box at the back of the cardboard creche and soon enjoyed the tinkling sound of "Silent Night." Stirring in me was a special sense I couldn't define. I just knew Christmas meant something wonderful.

The second I heard, "Janie, I'm finished. Come help me put these presents under the tree," I zipped to her side.

Soon, those bright-bowed treasures surrounded our tree. I waved my arms and turned in a circle. "Everything is so pretty!"

Mother put her arms around me. "Thanks for your help, Janie. Now I have some kitchen clean up to tend to," she added, leaving me in that beautiful moment.

I stretched out on the floor in front of the setting of Baby Jesus with Mary and Joseph and wound the music box again. That's when I heard a curious noise on the porch.

I jumped up as the front door swung open. In came my brother, Jim, in his Navy uniform. I opened my mouth to let out a squeal, but he tapped a finger to his lips. He scooped me up, and I hugged him as hard as I could. "Where's Mom?" he whispered.

"In the kitchen," I replied in his ear.

Down I went as he headed toward the back of the house. Of course, I trailed him.

I'll never forget seeing Mother's eyes as wide as could be and filled with tears. "Oh, Jim! You're home!"

"Only until tomorrow evening. I was able to get a brief pass to stop here before heading on to San Diego. That will be my duty station before shipping out."

Mother patted his arm. "Go sit and enjoy the Christmas glow. I'll bring you a cup of coffee."

He took my hand, and we went back to the living room. "You can't stay, Jimmy?" I frowned. "I don't want you to leave."

We sat together in an overstuffed chair tucked beside the tree. "Since I'm in the Navy, Little Miss, I have a job to do."

"Why can't you be in the Navy here?"

Mother came with the coffee, and my brother gave her a long look. "Shouldn't Judy be home soon, Mom?"

"Yes, she's working at Uncle Paul's store, but should be here anytime."

I giggled. "Just wait 'til she sees you."

Headlights and the sound of crunching gravel in the driveway signaled our sister's arrival. Jim got up, and I trembled inside.

My how Judy did holler! She dropped her packages in the chair by the door and moved like a lightning streak. Her arms flew around Jimmy, and she wept on his shoulder.

"I can't believe you're here tonight, Jim!"

At that, I inserted myself between them, enjoying all the happiness that embraced us.

Judy turned to Mother. "Did you know he would be home tonight?"

Smiling, Mother shook her head. "No, I didn't."

In that moment, my heart understood more about Christmas as love's warmth enveloped me.

When we heard the back door open, Jim said, "That's Dad. I'll sit here, and you all act real natural." He looked at me and smiled. "That means don't let him know I'm here, Janie. I want to surprise him too."

I climbed into the chair with him again. "I'll be real quiet here with you, Jimmy." He gave my hand a squeeze.

Mother went to greet Dad while Judy gathered her packages from the chair and placed them around the tree. I hardly breathed as I waited next to my brother — content to watch and listen.

Mother's words were muffled a bit, but I heard something about a visitor waiting in the living room. I covered my mouth to keep from snickering and gave Jimmy a little sister's admiring look.

I heard footsteps. "Dad's coming," I mouthed with a racing heart.

When he appeared at the arched doorway to the room, Dad stopped with a start. "Jim!"

My brother got up and wrapped his arms around my dad. I braced my hands at my side — *Dad's crying!*

I watched in amazement as Dad took his handkerchief out of his back pocket and dabbed his eyes, repeating, "Well, well."

Mother rested her hand on Dad's shoulder, and Judy bawled all the more. In that sweep of emotion, I danced, twirling around my family with childhood abandon.

Jim tucked me in bed that night. "You know, Santa will arrive when you're asleep, he said, pulling the comforter up under my chin.

I snickered. "I think he's already come."

Jim smoothed my bangs away from my eyes and turned to leave.

"You'll be here when I wake up, won't you?"

He paused at the doorway. "Yes, Little Miss. I want to see you open your present from me."

"What is it? Give me a clue!"

"No clues tonight," he said, waving a finger. "The quicker you go to sleep, the quicker Christmas morning will come."

He left the door cracked slightly, and I snuggled under the warmth of knowing my brother had come home for Christmas.

Winter sunlight peeped through my window. I heard Mother say, "Janie should be up soon."

I hopped out of bed. "I'm up!"

Oh, the joy of that Christmas morning! Judy played carols on the piano, and we all sang. I well remember Dad's bass voice, Jim's baritone, Judy and Mother's alto, and my high-pitched tones. Such a happy blend!

I don't recall what Christmas presents I opened that day, but toward the end of torn paper and tossed bows, my brother handed me the one from him. "Little Miss, before you open it, here are a couple of clues." He flashed me a big grin. "I'll be sailing on the wide open sea before long and be part of a crew onboard a big ship."

I gazed at him, wondering what "part of a crew" meant.

"I can't guess, Jimmy."

"Well, you can open your present without guessing. Go ahead." I pulled the glittery blue paper off and spied three wooden boats.

He sat down on the floor with me. "These are hand carved to look like the real Navy ones," he explained. "Look, this is a transport ship, and this is a submarine that travels under the sea."

Though I didn't understand all he said, my brother's words sounded exciting and important.

I held up the third one. "What's this little one?"

"That's called a tugboat, but it has a big job. It helps move large ships that get in trouble." I studied the smaller boat, turning it over in my hands. "Come on. I'll show you what I mean."

I followed him into the bathroom where he filled the sink with water. "What do you think these boats can do?"

"They'll float!" I announced, dropping each one in.

"Remember, I said a tugboat can help a big ship?" I nodded. "Let's pretend this transport can't move. It's engine won't run."

My brother brought the tug alongside the transport. "Watch." He pressed the tugboat to the ship's side, turning it around. Afterwards, he slipped the tug to the back and pushed the transport, making deep motoring sounds.

When the big ship shot forward through the water, I shouted, "Jimmy! It worked!"

"One more thing, Little Miss. Do you see the submarine?"

I spotted a dark shape under the water and lifted it up. "I found it!" His approving smile lifted me too.

"See this hole on top?" he said. "Now, push the sub down a little in the water."

The hole flooded, and the sub sank, overflowing our delightful time of make-believe that day.

As we tidied up the bathroom and set those handcrafted models on a shelf to dry, Jimmy said, "Little Miss, whenever you play with these when I'm gone, think about me sailing on my Navy boat."

My stomach churned to hear him talk about being gone, but I knew I'd always cherish the fun of our Christmas 'sailing adventures.'

Evening arrived, and the house quieted down. Laughter lessened, and I noticed my family spoke in lower tones. When Dad said, "The taxi is on its way, Jim. I'll ride with you to the train station," sadness welled up in me.

"Thanks Pop." Jimmy cleared his throat and looked at Mother. "This brief Christmas time here has been . . ."

Judy's eyes brimmed with tears. Jimmy hugged her and motioned for me. "Come here Little Miss."

I made a dash into his arms. "Thank you for my boats, Jimmy. I love them!"

Wrapping my arms tighter around his neck, I whispered, "I love you most of all."

Measureless wonder and love fills my heart even today, remembering that Christmas long ago. Its memory is forever mine!

21

The Christmas That Almost Wasn't

Judith Victoria Hensley

W hy in the world do you have your Christmas decorations up already?" a friend asked. "Halloween is barely behind us!"

It was true. I had never decorated my house so early or so thoroughly for Christmas. I usually waited until after Thanksgiving. Most of the time I waited until my birthday in December and let the festive decorations be part of my annual celebration.

Having been diagnosed with breast cancer in the fall of 2019 and with all of the treatments and surgery that came after, I had put no decorations out that year. Maybe I wanted to make up for it now and celebrate life a little bigger than I was physically able to do the year before. Or maybe it was because I had an inner nudge that said, "You've got to do it now."

I did my shopping early. In one weekend I had gifts for everyone. Ordinarily, they would have been stuck away until I hid them here and there under other people's Christmas trees. But not this time. They were purchased, wrapped, and distributed, for the most part, weeks earlier than usual.

From the attic I pulled down boxes and from the basement carried up containers that held many old, festive decorations that hadn't been out in years. My living room looked like a store's Christmas display!

I hung wreaths and garland. I put up a big artificial tree instead of the small pencil variety I had used for several years. A friend helped decorated every branch. I spread Christmas throws on the furniture and put lovely holiday flower arrangements in every place there was an empty spot. When I finished, I almost felt foolish. I had definitely gone overboard!

Still, it made me happy, and that was the point. I hoped that perhaps my aging parents, my son and his children and new wife, and my brother home from the college where he taught, all might spend Christmas dinner with me. My house that had been so drab and vacant of Christmas festivities the year before was going to make up for it on this go around.

At least that's what I thought.

When Mom called and told me that my eighty-nine-year-old dad had fallen and she had to call a neighbor to get him up, we were all frightened. That certainly was not like my dad. He and my mother had pastored a church into his eighties. She was the pianist and song leader, as well. They were spunky and self-reliant. If my mom had picked up the phone and called someone for help, she had to be desperate.

I went that day to check on them. I was so concerned that I left their house with the intention of coming home for a shower, packing up enough clothes to stay a few days, and heading back as soon as possible.

I took a shower, grabbed some personal items and called back to see if Mom wanted me to pick up anything from the store. No answer. I couldn't imagine why she wouldn't answer. I had been there only an hour before. I was sure she wasn't outside and doubted that they were both napping at that time of day.

I called again. Still no answer. I knew something was wrong but tried to calm myself. I had just seen them within the last hour. Maybe the telephones were down for some reason. I waited a few minutes and tried again. This time Mom answered in a panic and said Dad had fallen again, and she couldn't get him up. An ambulance was on the way.

Knowing my parents' attitude about calling an ambulance, I was certain it was a serious situation. Their home is about thirty minutes away from mine. I left my house and literally beat the ambulance to theirs. When Mom described what had happened, it sounded as if Dad may have had a seizure after he had fallen. He had been unable to respond to her or help himself in any way. She called a great nephew who is a nurse to come and help get Dad in a chair. He stayed with us while we waited for the ambulance to find the house.

The ambulance finally arrived and loaded Dad up. I followed it to the hospital. In the middle of Covid-19 and under extreme lockdown, no one should have been allowed to go back with him. However, he was disoriented, hard of hearing, and unable to answer their questions. They stuck him in one of the makeshift rooms that had been set up for Covid patients and allowed me to stay with him. It was about 3:15 A.M. when they finally put him in a room. We had spent hours in the ER. With Covid emergencies coming in, the staff was overwhelmed.

I wasn't allowed to go to the room on the hospital floor with Dad, so I went home to get some sleep. The next morning, I convinced Mom to come to my house for a night or two so we would be only five minutes from the hospital if we were needed. I went and picked her up, and brought her to my Christmas house. Her concern for Dad blocked out any joy she might have had about seeing the decorations, but at least she was there.

In less than an hour, the hospital was calling for us to come and pick Dad up. They had run several tests and hadn't found any kind of urgent need. He did not have Covid-19. We were instructed to take him to his regular doctor the following week.

Following up on those orders was the last time Dad left the house.

Hospice was called in immediately. Without a specific diagnosis, there was still the danger of him falling, and he quickly became unable to get out of bed without assistance. Mom and I stayed with him day and night in the family room downstairs where a hospital bed had been set up. My brother Mark came home from his job at the college at every opportunity he had.

As the weeks progressed, Mom and I both were exhausted, but I knew she was at her limit. Dad called for her constantly. He wanted her in the room with him. They had been married a few months shy of seventy years. They were a team, and he wanted his other half nearby.

Mom began to worry about decorating their house for Christmas. She pulled out a few little things to set about and abandoned the idea of formal decorations. I was glad my house was ready if Dad might improve enough to be taken there for Christmas dinner. We knew he was ill but we had no mental time frame for what was unfolding before us.

We were with Dad when he died on the morning of December 18. His passing was so peaceful that we weren't sure he was gone at first. With both of us by his bedside checking on him, he took one breath on planet earth and the next in heaven. It was like watching the peaceful sleep of a baby.

I realized Mom was shaking as she stood beside his bed, but I thought it was due to the emotions of the moment. I also knew at eighty-seven she was exhausted emotionally, mentally, and physically. I had no idea just how sick she was.

Mark had not been able to say good-bye to Dad. He couldn't get there until after the ambulance had taken Dad away and hospice had removed the hospital bed and all of the other equipment from the house. There was an empty spot where the bed had been and an empty spot in our hearts that could never be filled.

After Mark arrived and had been there for some time, I went home to shower, change, and get some sleep. We had major decisions ahead of us about funeral arrangements, but I needed rest first. I felt terrible. I had been up and down night after night. I hoped my own bed and a night's sleep would put things right again.

It was sad to come home to my empty Christmas house, but I was thankful I had the decorations up and gifts already purchased. I was glad I had taken care of those things early. It was a blessing and a worry lifted. I knew Mark would watch over Mom. My house would be ready for them when they came on Christmas day.

Mark called the next morning. Mom had told him she was sick so he called an ambulance in the middle of the night and she agreed to go in it. Alarms went off in both of us. This was not anything she would agree to lightly.

Through the night I had realized that I was also beyond exhaustion. Something terrible was wrong with me. I knew it.

Neither Mark nor I could get in to see Mom after he had to leave her in the Emergency Room. They took her to Covid ICU because she had Covid and double pneumonia.

I suspected it was what was wrong with me as well. I went straight to the outdoor Covid clinic . . . and tested positive. I was sent home with what seemed like a truckload of medicine and told to quarantine for fourteen days.

It was almost Christmas. Surely this couldn't be happening!

Mom was isolated in the hospital. I was seriously ill and isolated at home. Mark was at our parents' house alone. He and my son Jeremy had to make and take care of all the funeral arrangements. The funeral was held without Mom and I. It just didn't seem real.

There would be no Christmas for us, no family gathering, no Dad, no laughter, no meal, no presents. I grieved for the loss of my dad. I grieved for my mother in the hospital alone. I grieved for my brother at home alone. I grieved for myself alone at such a time.

Friends came and left food on a table outside my front door. They would call to say they were coming, and ring the doorbell when they arrived. Sometimes I got to wave good-bye from a distance. I was so weak it was all I could do to open the door and bring the food in. I had to force myself to eat and drink fluids.

A day or two after the funeral a winter storm hit. Mark had been on a mission to get clean clothes and personal items to Mom at the hospital, even though he couldn't get in to see her. I couldn't talk to her on the phone because her hearing aids were not working properly with the phone, and I was so weak my voice was barely a whisper. I wondered if they would do anything in the hospital for the patients at Christmas.

I kept calling the house to ask Mark what he'd found out, but there was no answer. With the winter storm in full swing, it could have been that the phone lines were down. I tried not to worry. There was nothing I could do for anyone, anyway. Covid sweats and fever were draining me completely. I lay in the dark of my house, too weak to eat, barely enough strength to get up to go to the bathroom.

Finally, the phone rang, and it was Mark. On his way home from the hospital he had wrecked the car directly across from the house. The car was on its side in the ditch, but once neighbors pulled him out of the vehicle, he only had to walk across the street to the house, to warmth, and to safety.

I turned on my Christmas tree lights that evening. After what could have been another heartbreak my brother's safety was a miracle. God had been so good to us. Dad had asked God to bring him home if he wasn't ever going to get better. He hadn't wanted to spend months or years in a hospital bed, unable to attend to his own needs. God honored his prayers and his passing was as gentle as ever could be.

Had Dad not passed when he did, Mom would never have agreed to leave him to go to the hospital for her own illness. Had Mark not been able to be here because of Christmas break, I would not have left Mom in her time of grief. Had the funeral not happened when it did, the winter storm would have overtaken the people coming and going to the ceremony.

The love of God, the goodness of God, broke through the darkness when I began to rehearse the distance my brother had traveled from the hospital to home in the raging weather. What would have been a half-hour drive in normal weather had taken him about two hours. He passed several wrecked cars on his way home. There were stretches without guardrails on the curvy mountainous road, and a long stretch beside a creek where he might have gone into the water without anyone knowing. There were miles with no houses and no help if he had wrecked along that stretch. There was much for which to be thankful.

As my Christmas lights twinkled, I saw the undelivered gifts and knew that not another living soul would be able to come into my house during the Christmas season because I was in Covid quarantine. Yet I did not feel alone.

I was so very thankful that God had spared my mom and my brother, and that I had survived breast cancer and would survive Covid. God loved us. He still had a plan for us. He still had a purpose for our lives, and we were not done with living.

The message of one Bible verse went through my mind repeatedly, "God so loved the world that He gave His only begotten Son that whosoever should believe on Him would not perish but have everlasting life." (John 3:16)

That is the true meaning of Christmas.

The decorations called out to me to rejoice in God's greatest gift of love to all of us, His son Jesus. Each night after that I made sure to turn on the Christmas lights and let their cheerfulness strengthen me.

I began to gain strength little by little from that evening on, first to my spirit, then to my body.

It was the Christmas that almost wasn't, but in the end we were all reminded of the true meaning of the day and how much we have to celebrate yet in this life. When we were able to gather together to share a meal and exchange gifts in the middle of January we certainly had a lot for which to be thankful . . . and a reminder that God's gift of love is present every day.

22

A Child in Red

Lori Ann Wood

I hold many memories of getting dressed for Midnight Mass as a child: the honor of being able to stay up past 9 P.M.; the anticipation of Christmas gifts edging ever closer as the minutes ticked by; the excitement of seeing the neighbor's silo adorned in lights like a flickering candle.

But one memory stands out now — the red lace head cover.

In those days we wore head coverings to church, mostly simple ones like a lace scarf or a crocheted doily. We had three of them in our house: a black mid-length one, a red circular cover, and a longer white veil. My mother, my sister, and I rotated those options according to our outfits. Mom would quickly choose one for each of us as we were leaving, and fasten it to our hair with a bobby pin. I always hoped for the long white veil. It made me feel like a princess, extending my short brown pixie haircut with glorious lace. This particular Christmas my dress was mostly white, so I thought I had a good chance. My older sister's colorful dress could support any of the three. I closed my four-year-old eyes and waited for Mom to pin on my cover. When I opened them, I glanced in the mirror to see it was the red one, my least favorite.

It threatened to ruin my Christmas.

Even then I considered red a loud, obnoxious color. It screams for attention . . . and usually gets it. I was painfully shy, and the red cover made me self-conscious. Sometimes I could take it in stride by forgetting what was up there, out of my own sight. But for Christmas? I sulked, mostly secretly. The last thing I wanted was to be noticed.

As an adult I saw *Schindler's List*, a black and white film set during the Holocaust. The only color seen in the film is an occasional image of a little girl in a red coat. We see the little coat hiding under a bed from the Nazis. In a group of playing children. In a mass of people being herded into freight cars. And finally, we see a flicker of red in a cart carrying dead bodies.

The little girl in the film didn't want to be seen either. But by being seen, by being noticed by Schindler, she made a difference in a larger cause. She made the bigger story become a personal one.

Not everyone agreed with the use of the red coat icon in *Schindler's List*. Movie reviewer Philip Martin said, "I did not like the way Spielberg spotlighted the girl in the red coat; it seems unnecessarily melodramatic and condescending in that it implied that the audience needed to latch on to an individual tragedy beyond the larger crime of the Holocaust."

Amazingly, that is precisely what God does. He latches on to each of our personal stories as if we are the only one in the movie. Not someone beyond the larger story, but an integral part of it.

The concept of "an audience of one" conveys that we should live our lives as if only God is watching. To take it a step further, perhaps in some ways God parents us as if we were His only child. He literally has all the time in the world for each one of us. And against the backdrop of this dark world, He sees each of us individually, perfectly, clearly.

Frederick Buechner said of Schindler's girl in red: "God sees each of us as the child in the red coat, just as His eye is on the sparrow."

The words of Jesus are for the world and yet for me alone, *"Aren't five sparrows sold for two pennies? Yet not one of them is forgotten in God's sight."* (Luke 12:6 HCSB)

These may seem like strange sentiments for the Christmas season. But it is the essence of the love the Father had for us individually in sending His Son into this world. His deep love bled out in red for each of us every day, felt most keenly in times of deep distress.

Remembering the little girl in red helps us as we struggle about our place, our importance, our purpose. When we are tempted to let the "why" of painful living enter our minds and then tumble from our lips, Christ's red covering gives us assurance of protection, outside of our understanding.

From One Tiny Babe to one tiny person — one tiny person in a mass of warring politics and world hunger, global pandemics and garnered wind farms. He can see us in all His plans. He walks with us and works within us. Every single day. Just that one little child in red.

At Mass that Christmas Eve, the church was packed with holiday visitors and returning parishioners. Our customary pew was filled when we arrived, so we traipsed up the tight staircase to the choir loft for seats. Following the final carol, I got up quickly and left a mitten in my chair.

My hands discovered the lone mitten in my coat pocket. When I slipped back for its mate, I got separated from my family. Everyone looked unfamiliar, and so much taller than I was. Panic started to set in. Suddenly, I felt my mother's firm hand on top of my head, steering me. Instantly, I knew it was the red cover that had identified me in the elbow-to-elbow crowd.

As I matured, I realized the red head covering I wore that Christmas Eve was not a mark of shame. It was a mark of claim. It didn't save me from the pain of getting lost, but it helped me get Home.

I am His, bought with the blood. Borne by the Babe.

I see that red covering differently now.

23

Celebrating Christ
at Christmas

by Bill Tinsley

At this time of year, our thoughts turn to celebrating Christmas. It is a time for decorating our homes and erecting the Christmas tree with all its glitz and glamour. Then there is the shopping. We go to the malls and are greeted with the sights and sounds of the season. We're drawn in by the sights of Christmas decorations while Christmas carols play, enticing us to shop. With list in hand, we set out to conquer. "On sale! Marked down! Clearance! Fifty percent off!" entices us into individual stores.

We review the names on our lists and check off those of family and friends as our shopping bags fill with gifts we have thoughtfully purchased for each individual.

As we meander through the mall, our attention is captivated by the main man. There he is in all his colorful glory — Santa Claus! A line of parents and children wait to tell Santa what they want for Christmas. As he sits upon his throne the attending elves pass out candy canes to each child.

Arms loaded with gifts, we get in our cars and head home. Hopefully there is a tinge of crisp coolness in the air to reinforce the sense of the season. Driving home, we pass by houses adorned with colorful lights and lawn ornaments; each home, it seems is trying to outdo the other.

Please do not think that this description is a protest against the Christmas season! I truly love this time of year. My house glows with the lights of the season and the ornaments on display for all to see stand second to none . . . at least in my own estimation.

However, I would ask you, as you poured over the names on you Christmas list, was a name missing?

Is Jesus on your list?

Although we should celebrate Jesus in our lives every day, we set apart this time of year to add extra emphasis to His birth. This is the season to celebrate Christ, not Christmas.

Our great enemy, Satan, doesn't care if you celebrate Christmas, as long as you don't celebrate Jesus Christ. Satan figured out more than two thousand years ago that he couldn't defeat Jesus and that Jesus is the chosen Son of God sent into the world so mankind might be reconciled to Him.

In many ways Satan has stolen Christmas from Christians.

"Merry Christmas" is replaced with "Happy Holidays."

As you observe this Christmas season, if Christmas has replaced Christ in your life, allow the Holy Spirit to recapture the essence of the season. In the midst of all the excitement of the holidays seek ways to make Jesus the center of your celebration. Find ways for you and your family to rejoice in the birth of our Savior.

A few ways my family strives to keep Christ in Christmas is by reading the Christmas story from the Gospels on Christmas Eve and lighting a candle as we sing Happy Birthday to the King. If you decorate the outside of your home, include something to show the world that Jesus is the reason for celebrating Christmas.

Many years ago we started a tradition of installing a twelve-foot cross on the top story of our house. It's trimmed in white lights and a star rests on top, for us it signifies that Jesus was brought into this world to suffer and die on a cross for our sins so we could be reconciled to the Father.

The cross was my wife's idea, and I must confess that at the time I was afraid of what the neighbors would think. I, myself, was in danger of replacing Christ with Christmas. Setting my fears aside, I built and erected the cross.

Now, the sight of the lighted cross is visible for all who turn onto our street to see. You cannot help but see it shining in all its glory. This one act of keeping Christ in Christmas has had an effect on people I've never even met. I remember a few years ago, I was running late getting the decorations up. It was only a couple of weeks until Christmas Day. As I hoisted up the cross on the second story of our house, a car pulled up and a lady emerged. Once again as a weak vessel of God, my first thought was that she was going to criticize me. I cannot tell you the joy that filled my heart when all she said was, "I was so afraid that you were not going to put up the cross this year."

Brothers and sisters in Christ, we have no idea how our actions — be they large or small — might affect another person's walk with Christ!

This holiday season, let the light and life of Christ shine in your life and use you to spread hope to the hopeless, joy to the sorrowful, and salvation to the lost. Keep Christ as the foundation of your Christmas.

Even so, come quickly Lord Jesus.

24

Silent Night, Pandemic Night

Mel Tavares, DMin.

Silent night, pandemic night. Christmas Eve, a time of family gathering and festivities, was celebrated with just the two of us. None of the seven kids, their spouses, or nine grandkids arrived to decorate gingerbread cookies, watch Christmas movies, and open presents.

As the sun dropped and I bent to turn the tree lights on, the familiar emotion of self-pity rose from within my grieving heart. "Just the two of us," I mused. "It reminds me of how Mary and Joseph must have felt on that first Christmas."

Tears welled in my eyes as I thought of how lonely Mary must have been that evening. I closed my eyes and let my mind drift to the stable scene of long ago. An outsider looking into the sacred setting, my imagination so intense I thought I heard Mary praying, "God, why has my family forsaken me? Why don't they believe me? Rejection is so painful, and I am all alone on a day intended to be filled with family and friends celebrating and rejoicing together." I saw Joseph reach over, wipe the tears from her cheek, and put a reassuring arm around her shoulders.

The brush of his hand seemed so real, and as I opened my eyes, I realized it was my husband's finger brushing the tears away from my cheeks. As he bent to kiss my forehead, he gently asked, "Why are you sad? Is it because the kids and grandkids aren't here tonight? Just a moment ago, you were smiling and happy."

His words rang true. The entirety of 2020 had been filled with emotions that seemed to slide from one side of the pendulum to the other, happy to sad, glad to mad, peaceful to fearful. One moment thankful the kids and grandkids were healthy and Covid free, the next moment having a pity party over not seeing each other.

My mind drifted back to Mary, there in the stable on that silent, holy night. No friends or family around, yet joy filled the stable. There were no fresh-baked cookies, no feast prepared to celebrate the birth of Christ, the Savior of the world.

"What do you want to do about our Christmas Eve dinner?" my husband asked, jolting me back to the present.

"I bought lobster as always," I replied. "If I can't be in Maine with my family, at least I can eat my Maine lobster."

Determined not to let the pandemic steal my Christmas joy, I turned on the Christmas carols and found the lobster pot. "This is my guilty pleasure," I said, justifying the expense of eating an imported lobster. "It's been a long year, and lobster is a perfect Christmas Eve dinner for two."

For an hour, I bustled around the kitchen, making a salad, fresh biscuits, and Maine potatoes to go with my Maine lobster. Strains of a choir singing "Silver bells, it's Christmas time in the city. Children laughing, people passing, meeting smile after smile" drifted through the air. My happy mood dipped low and I frowned, missing the smiles on the city streets this year. Instead, masked people passed quickly by, eyes averted. This year, I saw few shoppers rushing home with their treasures; most had ordered online. This Christmas Eve Santa's sleigh had been replaced by delivery trucks.

The loud buzz of the timer jolted me back to my kitchen. "The lobster smells so good," I said aloud as if the family could hear me. Quickly, I pulled the biscuits from the oven, melted the butter in the microwave, and pulled the lobsters from the pot.

My husband's handsome face softened in the candlelight as we spoke of each of seven households filled with our kids and grandkids. "I'm sure they love all the gifts we've dropped off or mailed to them." Again, a tear slipped down my cheek, much as I tried to blink it away and focus on my lobster and all of the positives in our collective lives. "Hey, do you think we could maybe FaceTime some of them later?" I inquired.

Again, the soft brush of his finger wiped the tear trickling down my cheek. "Of course."

Hope filled the room once again. If nothing else, the pandemic taught us all resilience and the necessity to adapt to change. I thought back to Mary, giving birth in a stable. Most young girls dream of the day they get married and later discover they are pregnant. Mary's story didn't happen the way she had dreamed of, yet she adapted. As others spoke out against her, resilience was required. Even then, she probably envisioned having the baby in the comfort of home, only to discover change was necessary when she needed to travel to Bethlehem. While I imagine how challenging it would have been for me to give birth to one of my children in a stable, perhaps Mary accepted and adapted readily, having already been through nine months of challenges.

"Nine months!" I exclaimed aloud. "We've been dealing with this pandemic for nine months already!" My husband and I stared at one another, lobster claws in hand. I continued reminiscing through nine months of challenges we'd endured. "Do you remember the day officials said Covid would last two weeks? Ha! That was nine months ago. Like millions of others, we've endured untold hardships. The worst, though, is missing out on celebrating birthdays, anniversaries, milestones in each of our lives. And now we can't celebrate Christmas together. I pray this pandemic is over soon."

Just as I was licking the last bit of butter off my fingers, my phone buzzed. The grandkids were calling. *I'm so thankful for the months of FaceTiming,* I thought as I pressed the button and the video clicked on. For the next two hours, we chatted with one household and then the next. Most of us opted to open pre-delivered gifts in keeping with Christmas Eve tradition.

Amid the chorus of "Good night, I love you, go to sleep, talk to you tomorrow, and Merry Christmas" was the overwhelming feeling of gratitude, that while Christmas Eve was very different on this pandemic night, it had turned out to be anything but silent.

"We can't forget one final tradition!" Talking with the family nearly caused me to forget to put the year's ornament on the tree. I reached into a box delivered just two days before and pulled out my new favorite ornament. "We will forever treasure this 2020 ornament as a reminder of all we've endured and overcome." We both laughed as we hung it on the branch and looked at the icons on it, having nearly forgotten the Great Toilet Paper Shortage, the homemade masks, the hunt for bleach and hand sanitizer, curbside pickups and home deliveries, and Zoom calls.

The familiar scent of eggnog filled my nostrils as I poured two glasses and smiled contentedly at my husband. "In a world filled with chaos, it is calm and bright here in the living room on this pandemic Christmas Eve night."

He smiled, his eyes twinkling much like those I'd seen as a young child spying on the man in the red suit. "It's a different kind of Christmas this year, but I have to confess I am enjoying this evening home alone with you."

The clock struck midnight as we climbed the stairs to settle in for a long winter's nap. As I drifted to sleep, I thought again of Mary and Joseph and baby Jesus in the silent, holy night, and then of our silent pandemic night. The truth is, none of us had spent the night alone. Mary and Joseph were in a noisy stable amid a crowded city, and I had spent the night celebrating Jesus's birth virtually with my family.

25

New Address

Rita Klundt

It's the night before Christmas. We're in the new house.
Not a creature is stirring, not even a mouse.
The stockings are hung in the hallway with care.
No fireplace, no mantel, no chimney is there.

We're sleepy and nestled all snug in our beds.
No sugar plums dancing around in our heads.
No Christmas pajamas. No long pointy cap.
But we're all settled in for a long winter's nap.

Tonight on the lawn if we hear an odd clatter.
We're too tired to leap up or care what is the matter.
If outside the window, we do see a flash,
We've yet to hang curtains or blinds. What's a sash?

The moon reflects brightly on new fallen snow.
It covers a lawn where the grass failed to grow.
We wish to our wondering eyes would appear,
New furniture, some draperies, but please no reindeer.

The geese on the lake are still lively and quick.
When they stayed for the winter we named one Saint Nick.
Our neighbors are giving them plenty to eat.
Each day after sunrise they come for their treat.

Now Dasher. Now Dancer. Now Prancer and Vixen!
On Comet! On Cupid! On Donner and Blitzen!
Get off of my porch and stay off my new wall.
Now dash away. Dash away. Dash away all!

Our request goes unanswered by these spoiled birds.
They continue to leave us a yard full of turds.
These guests, uninvited, force tolerant hosts.
Christmas dinner? We spotted a fat goose to roast.

So, back to attempting that long winter's nap.
Our eyelids are droopy. The presents are wrapped.
Our package arrived from across many states.
The cookies and fudge grace a glass Christmas plate.

What are we forgetting? Is something undone?
No gift is forgotten. No, not even one.
Then why can't we sleep and get much needed rest?
Wait! We need to thank God for the way we've been blessed.

We start naming blessings. Those geese being one.
By wee hours of the morning, we'll never be done.
In a couple of hours the bright sun will rise.
We're tired and sleepy, but can't close our eyes.

It's now Christmas morning. Our hearts celebrate.
The Messiah is born, both tiny and great.
God's grace and His purpose came down in plain sight.
Merry Christmas to all! It has been a good night.

26

An Unforgettable Christmas Aeromedical Evacuation

Robert B. Robeson, LTC (USA Ret)

The chatter of three separate and distinct machine guns filled the cockpit of our unarmed, UH-1H (Huey), medical evacuation helicopter. It rang in my ears that Christmas Thursday morning in 1969, south of Da Nang, South Vietnam, and tore at my insides like a rusty knife.

Another aircraft commander, and close friend, had asked me for a favor. He wanted to switch our field standby duties at Landing Zone Hawk Hill, about thirty-two miles south of Da Nang along Highway 1, during the Christmas ceasefire arranged in Paris. I'd been shot down once and had three other birds shot up by enemy fire in the previous five and a half months of continuous action with the 236th Medical Detachment (Helicopter Ambulance). It sounded like an excellent opportunity for some R&R — rest and relaxation — during the negotiated truce.

The reddish mud encompassing our home away from home at Hawk Hill was still mushy from the night's dew. We were supporting elements of the U.S. American Division, U.S. Marine Corps, U.S. Special Forces (Green Berets), allied troops — South Vietnamese, South Korean, Australian — and the Vietnamese civilian population. All of the units were in defensive positions. I'd just completed a thorough preflight, had set up the cockpit for day operations, and was lazily taking in the early morning sunshine. That's when our radio-telephone operator ran toward me from the battalion aid station. He was waving a long, white mission sheet.

"You've got an urgent insecure mission for nine ARVNs (South Vietnamese Army soldiers). All of them hit by small arms. Shot up pretty bad. Their compound was attacked about ten to fifteen minutes ago. They've taken more small arms and some mortars since then." He paused for a second. "No Americans are at the pickup site. They'll radio-relay through an interpreter from a position about ten miles away."

"This is a joke. Right?" I asked. He shook his head.

"How come I always have to deal with the ten percent who never get the word?"

"Merry Christmas, sir."

Within seconds I'd plotted the grid coordinates on my map, the rest of my crew had arrived, and we were airborne. Our destination was Barrier Island, a historically dangerous stretch of white sand and small villages nestled against the picturesque South China Sea, east of Hawk Hill.

My stomach knotted as we neared the pickup site. It was a silent premonition. At that moment, there was no doubt in my military mind that this warm and pleasant Christmas morning — much like it may have been in Bethlehem nearly two thousand years before — would be a special one. I talked to the American infantry advisor ten miles from the pickup site. He gave me an update on the condition of the patients, direction of the last ground fire, and where they wanted us to land. Then I asked him to relay a request to pop a canister of colored smoke.

The last reported fire had come from the southwest. I decided to drop down from two thousand feet to the northeast and come in low-level on the deck. That way, I could keep the outpost situated atop a small hill between myself and any potential incoming fire.

They popped smoke and we correctly identified the color. Then

I began my zigzagging tactical approach. We were in a forty-five-hundred-feet-per-minute descent and airspeed had built to a redlined one hundred twenty knots. That's when I distinctly remember glancing inside to check the instruments while falling through eight hundred feet. As my altimeter swept past seven hundred feet, staccato bursts of machine gun fire immediately triggered the burglar alarm in my central nervous system. Bullets began to splatter throughout the cargo compartment and cockpit, tearing through the tender and vulnerable underbelly of our bird. It was a familiar sound, one you never forget once you've experienced it. It reminded me of fire through a forest when underbrush is dry and laurel crackles.

In an instant, I felt like a baby waiting for a diaper change. There was no doubt we were seriously damaged. Fumes from our JP-4 jet fuel filled the aircraft. A fuel cell was obviously riddled and we were trailing a thin mist of flammable JP-4. Even today, all I have to do to bring back this experience is to close my eyes. The images of that mission appear before me, instantly, like the black spots you see after looking at a welding torch.

"Painful" is too bland a word to capture the twang of that agony as the reality of the moment dawned in my brain. War had suddenly become complicated and personal again.

Strange things occur in cockpits in combat, and crewmembers have a habit of talking about subjects the average person might tend to repress. My copilot was a warrant officer straight from flight school with barely two-hundred-twenty total hours of flight time. He'd already heard numerous war stories from the other veteran pilots.

"How does it feel to get shot up?" he'd asked as we were on our way to the pickup site. He sounded a little like a youngster on the way to his first dental appointment for a tooth filling.

That wasn't the typical question a new pilot posed on the way to his initial insecure mission. Not when strangers could be waiting to use our red crosses for bull's-eyes.

"It's difficult to describe," I'd replied. "Someday, if it ever happens to you . . . you'll know what I mean." (Less than four months later, he and another crew would win Silver Stars after being shot down at Hiep Duc with ten patients aboard.)

Pulling up sharply from the dive and seeking the temporary safety of a higher altitude, I asked each person over the intercom if he was okay. My crew chief reported that a round had kicked his leg into the air, making a half-inch indentation in the deck where his foot had been. He wasn't hurt. Our medic was uninjured, too.

My rookie copilot was silently transfixed, as though in a hypnotic trance. He was staring intently at the instrument panel. After asking him twice if he was all right, and receiving no reply, I reached over with my left hand and jostled his shoulder. He didn't say a word . . . only nodded his head affirmatively.

"Well, that's what it feels like," I reminded him. "Call Hawk Hill and tell them to have another bird flown out from Da Nang so we can get back out there before those guys die on us." I could tell from his facial expression and body language that he wasn't anymore excited about going back than I was.

For a brief moment, there was a mountain of self-pity on my part. I couldn't think of a more miserable way to die than during a supposed wartime cease-fire on Christmas Day — my first Christmas of married life. I knew it wouldn't be fair to my wife who'd just lost her father, at forty-six years of age, not long before. What kind of a Christmas present would that be for her?

We flew toward Hawk Hill with jet fuel spilling out behind us . . . a potential airborne torch ready to be lit by any inadvertent spark of misfortune. We lost two-hundred fifty pounds of fuel on the seven-minute flight back.

As soon as our skids touched the ground at Hawk Hill, I chopped the throttle and we all bailed out in different directions. When the blades stopped, we cautiously returned to inspect the damage. There were nineteen entry holes: eight in one fuel cell, six in the cockpit, and the rest in the cargo compartment. Not one of them had hit anyone. We might not have been around to take inventory if the enemy had been using tracers.

JP4 was still draining from the belly of our bird. A huge pool collected as we watched. Our self-sealing fuel tanks couldn't have been expected to work efficiently when the "shot group" was so concentrated in a six-inch circle in one fuel cell.

My Christmas dinner consisted of a tasteless, cold turkey sandwich. It was nervously consumed while another helicopter was ferried out for our use from Da Nang.

We could have backed out then. Nobody probably would have blamed us. There were no Americans at the pickup site. The landing zone was still insecure. We weren't going to get helicopter gunship cover. All of these *could* have been excuses for turning down the mission.

Sitting in the aid station near the radio shack, I quietly reflected on those nine Asian youngsters fighting to live. They were lying out there in an exposed outpost, under siege. They were probably wondering if the Americans cared enough to "hang-it-out" for them a second time. We were their only hope and link to medical care and, perhaps, life itself. After only a few months of war, I had already recognized the strong emotional bond that is formed among soldiers, regardless of nationality. We shared the same privations, hardships, and dangers of combat. If I'd have been in their position, I'd have wanted someone to be there for me, too.

Having been raised in the home of a Protestant minister, the spiritual dimensions of my life and faith had always been strong. Maybe that's why one question surfaced to dominate my thinking at that point. It seemed to come out of nowhere. *Do you care enough about the freedoms these troops are fighting for — and their wounds — to die trying to evacuate them?*

Then a passage of scripture filtered through my mind from my biblical upbringing. It was by James, the brother of Jesus. *"Consider it pure joy, my brothers, whenever you face trials . . . because you know the testing of your faith develops perseverance."* This is found in James 1:2-3 (NIV).

In those brief moments of reflection and contemplation, I determined that this mission wasn't anywhere near over. It wouldn't be until we evacuated all of our patients, ran out of aircraft, or were permanently put out of commission.

On the return flight in a new bird, I decided to come in low-level from the east a couple of miles out. We requested continuous smoke so we wouldn't lose the landing zone.

Redlining my airspeed indicator, I snuggled down a few feet above terra (very) firma. Weaving back and forth across the mostly flat terrain, I used small hills and tree lines to hide behind as much as possible. Nearing their smoke from the east, we again encountered a barrage of small arms and machine gun fire. Staying on the deck, I swung back to the south like we were leaving the area. It felt like what a rabbit must experience when it blunders onto an active military firing range.

When the firing ceased, I immediately did a hairy, 180-degree turn and headed due north. I don't know if this perseverance surprised the "bad guys." We were on short final for the purple smoke before small arms fire again erupted behind us.

Our nine patients were hurriedly tossed aboard. Then I flew out, low-level, the same way we'd come in and did a cyclic climb to two thousand feet. We escaped without any "hits" in our second aircraft, even though the landing zone had apparently been surrounded.

At altitude, paralleling the coast north toward Da Nang, I turned in my armored seat to see how our patients were doing. All had multiple gunshot wounds. One ARVN, shot in an arm and leg, was slumped against the bulkhead behind my copilot's seat. Our eyes met briefly when I turned around. There was no facial expression, merely a distinct and formal bow of his head in my direction. I believe he knew what it had taken to evacuate them. It was a "thank you" from a fellow soldier that

I've never forgotten. This was the greatest Christmas present a medevac pilot could ever receive. Helping others in great need during difficult times was something I'd always dreamed of being involved in, from as far back as I could remember. Now these patients we had finally evacuated would have another opportunity to fulfill their own dreams.

We hadn't done anything extraordinary, considering other soldiers, other wars, and the long course of human history. We hadn't done anything that thousands of other soldiers on the ground and in the air hadn't accomplished before or after us in that Southeast Asian war. We all knew what it meant to struggle to stay alive and be a part of the front lines in armed conflict, not on the sidelines. And we intimately understood that combat is a blend of extreme violence, gentleness, caring, hope, faith, prayer, a unique sense of the "nearness" of death, and continuous dreaming that it would soon be over.

The central point of this mission involved hope and love. These two words are really the twin messages of Christmas. They ultimately rest on a social contract that calls on us to take risks for others.

This Christmas message of hope and love plays out in our daily lives through the willingness and selflessness of one human being to care about another. It provides someone an opportunity to survive, to grow, and have a chance for a better life. The greatest gift of all is that the one taking the risk expects nothing in return.

The campfire of that special combat experience has dwindled to crimson coals. I'm seventy-nine years of age now, but when Christmas rolls around each year I always recall the precarious moments involved in those two special evacuation missions.

What I discovered that Christmas day was that a growth of character is possible through life-and-death struggles and in taking risks for others. It's always appropriate to help someone who's a little more lost and hurting than we are. This is because hope, love, and dreaming about the possibilities in life are what keep humanity going. And that's what this season has always been about . . . even in a combat zone.

27

Black Cookies and God Colors

Lynn U. Watson

Add Black Spritz Cookies to the list of weird for 2020.

Our granddaughters join me to bake and decorate cookies every year. The cookie menu always includes Spritz cookies. It's been a holiday tradition in my family for the sixty-five plus years I remember. My grandmother and mother included me in the fun. I included my own children. The last twelve or thirteen years I have included my daughter's precious girls. This year, 2020, would be no exception — no pandemic would halt the tradition.

Except, in an effort to be sure we had really green dough for the Christmas trees, I added an extra dash (or two, or ten) of green food color. The result: We had black dough!

After deciding nothing was wrong with the food colors, we proceeded with our Christmas baking. We joked the cookies would be cinders or coals for naughty children. We considered the fact that recently DIY home improvement shows were encouraging a trend toward one or more charcoal or black walls in their home renovations.

Would our cookies be trendy? One thing those Christmas tree cookies would not be was green.

Later, I took to social media sharing about our silly baking mis-adventure. The images were met with fun reactions. Someone suggested the cookies came from the Black Forest. Fun explanation to me, since the main character in a novel I've been working on hails from the area of southwest Germany, close to those real-life fairy-tale-like woods.

With smiles on our faces, we had pushed the black dough into the press, squeezed the trigger, and watched the black trees line our cookie sheets. The girls added colorful sprinkles and candies, each trying to outdo the other in creativity. The bright decorative touches they added popped boldly on the very dark backgrounds. The black trees showed off their colors! They reminded me of one of my favorite passages.

> *Here's another way to put it: You're here to be light, bringing out the God-colors in the world. God is not a secret to be kept. We're going public with this, as public as a city on a hill. If I make you light-bearers, you don't think I'm going to hide you under a bucket, do you? I'm putting you on a light stand. Now that I've put you there on a hilltop, on a light stand—shine! Keep open house; be generous with your lives. By opening up to others, you'll prompt people to open up with God, this generous Father in heaven.* Matthew 5:14-16 (MSG)

God has certainly given us opportunities in the bleakness of 2020, and moving forward into a most unpredictable future, to be shining lights of His love. The beauty of His Spirit within us empowers us to draw others to Him. May the God-colors of Christmas (and every day) seen from your life be those lived in kindness and God's love, more than from the festive wrappings under your tree or the glowing lights on your home. Or even from brightly-trimmed black Christmas tree cookies.

Merry Christmas from our home to yours!

Spritz Cookies

Ingredients

1 pound salted butter

1 tbsp shortening

2 eggs

1½ cups sugar

1 tbsp vanilla

1 tsp baking powder

5 cups flour

Instructions

1. Combine all ingredients and mix well.
2. Divide and add food color as desired. (We used paste food colors.)
3. Place dough in cookie press with desired disc shapes.
4. Press onto cookie sheet. (We *do not* recommend using dark cookie sheets.)
5. Decorate with sprinkles, candy decos, cinnamon hearts, colored sugars.
6. Bake at 350° for 8-10 minutes.
7. Allow to sit for a minute before removing from cookie sheet to cooling rack.
8. Cool cookie sheets between each baking.
9. Store in airtight container.

28

Christmas Joy

Shirl Hart

C an you come?" my sister Joy asked. She knew I would. When we were young we'd shared only two family Christmases together. When Mother died we were dispatched in different directions. We were adults before we met again. Now, Joy's phone call meant I'd be going to celebrate what doctors said would be her last Christmas.

At Joy's upstate New York farm home, I knocked and opened the door. I knew from past experiences that a handshake is an age-old sign of goodwill and respect. If you refrain, the one you have rebuffed will no doubt take offense — even if it's a sable collie like the one that greeted me. Four other canines, waiting with paws extended, watched my awkward movement.

"Shake their paws," my sister Joy's weak voice commanded from her hospice bed. "I have checked. Shaking hands with five dogs is harmless as long as you wash with soap and hot water and don't touch your eyes, nose, mouth, or me before you reach the sink."

"Merry Christmas, little one," she wheezed. "Welcome to animal hospice. You will be surprised at how much they will help you."

"I brought you a gift," I said. I handed her a package of yellowed letters addressed to her in neat handwriting.

"Mother's letters to me while she was hospitalized? I've never seen these." Her voice grew stronger and she wiped a tear. "Where did you get them?"

"They were among Dad's things when he died." I checked the

moisture of the Christmas cactus blooming above her bed.

On my way to the kitchen to find water for the plant, five dogs followed. I stopped. "What's with you guys?" They took a polite step back in unison and sat.

Joy had placed her letters on the nightstand by the time the dogs followed me back to her bedside. She reminisced. A journey that lasted until her final hours.

"All my life, I missed Mother." Joy took my hand. "I'm sorry you were too young to remember how loving and good she was. She met me at the school bus stop every night and listened to my endless chatter. She played games with us, kissed our bumps and bruises away. I loved her so much. These letters are the best gift you could ever give me."

She fell asleep with the letters stacked on her nightstand.

Lakefront snow swirled past the windows while I sat on the edge of her bed massaging her arms with five furry helpers dozing at my feet,

Joy's dogs tolerated no neglect. If I slept too soundly and didn't hear her call, a cole, pointy nose aroused me. If she turned over and exposed her back, they yanked on my comforter. They monitored my administration of morphine, and sat at attention with eyes bright and steady during hospice workers' visits. Twenty feet padded after me each time I left the room. And twenty feet accompanied me on my return.

Joy read and reread Mother's letters for a few days until her eyes lost focus. No longer able to read, she touched them reverently.

"What about Dad? He gave both of us away. Are you bitter?"

"I forgave him." I didn't elaborate on the peace I experienced many years ago.

"Me, too," she said.

She changed the subject. "Will Ann visit this afternoon? Wednesday is her usual day."

Ann, an old friend known for her promptness, arrived on time. An hour later she glanced at her watch. "Almost five. I'd better go. I'll see you next week."

"I won't be here," Joy answered. Ann nodded and let herself out.

Only seconds later, my sister sat up in bed and stretched out her arms with a radiant smile on her face, her voice filled with excitement and wonder. "Mother! I am so glad to see you."

I froze in place. Outside people wished each other Merry Christmas and sang songs about peace and joy. Inside an old New York farmhouse I saw nothing but happiness on my sister's face. I witnessed it in awe.

At the sound of Joy's raised voice, the dogs streaked to her bedside and reared up on their haunches.

"She is more than just okay. See for yourselves." I lifted five dogs, one at a time, onto the bed with Joy. They snuggled around her, their little faces solemn.

Did I think our Mother visited my sister before Joy died?

Would the dogs shake hands with me when I left for my Florida home?

The answers are yes and yes.

29

A Promise Kept

Bonnie Lasley Harker

'Twas a starry night,
A stable quiet,
A doting mother;
A watchful father.

Prophets foretold Him.
Hope had long grown dim.
Now God's Son was born
To a world forlorn.

No room at the inn
For His life to begin.
It was only on hay
Where Messiah lay.

Jesus, Prince of Peace,
Brought men to their knees.
Their hearts filled with joy
O'er this baby boy.

The rescue for all
Lay in a cow's stall.
His birth led to others,
Sisters and brothers.

God's heart was such
And His love so much,
That He sent our King
Eternal life to bring.

What a wondrous sight
In the stable's light.
God's promise was kept
While the baby slept.

30

Long Distance Christmas

By Barb Latta

A traveling germ changed everyone's world in 2020. The year evolved into a parenthesis in time where we lived in social paralysis. While this virus did have some effect on my family's holiday that year, it wasn't totally the disease's fault.

My husband's job at an Army base near Atlanta, Georgia was coming to an end for that location. The company he was employed with had two options: Fort Drum, New York, or South Korea.

I wasn't too keen on moving across the ocean for a designated time period, but I also didn't want to face winter in Fort Drum, New York. Korea has winter too, but not the harshness of the season at the Canadian border.

So, we set off on an adventure halfway around the world. We said a tearful good-bye to our son, daughter-in-law, and granddaughter, who live in Florida. But we looked forward to visiting our other son, who worked in Hong Kong. We hoped our closer location to him would make connecting easier.

We arrived in September of 2020. After our required two-week quarantine ended, we moved into housing and settled into the new culture as much as possible considering we couldn't go anywhere. Churches were closed. Virus restrictions shut down restaurants, tours were impossible to take, and wearing masks was a requirement.

Sign-in sheets were at every building we entered on Camp Humphreys, the Army base where my husband, Ken, was now assigned to work.

Name, phone number, address, and temperature were recorded for contact tracing.

Streets resembled those of western ghost towns in cowboy movies. As cases of Covid eased, some businesses were allowed to reopen. Restaurants and coffee shops could only serve take-out but at least that was something. Thankfully, the commissary and PX on the base were open; that was the main place military people could get food and supplies — but there were limits on the number of bodies who could shop at the same time.

Even Santa had to wear a mask.

With the scarcity of toilet paper back in the United States, I thought about buying packages of tissue and using it for gifts. No one would stand in the customer service line to return that present. It was a highly coveted commodity everyone could use. But I wasn't sure if I put that on a customs form if it would get intercepted due to need before it made it to its destination. Besides, it was a little bulky for mailing.

The small apartment we had rented didn't allow space for a tree, so I used a corner and put up a ribbon as a substitute to oversee the gifts Ken and I gave each other.

As Christmas grew closer, we knew we wouldn't be with our son who worked in Hong Kong. The quarantine made travel impossible for him.

Our family was separated by three locations, so our only option for togetherness on Christmas Day was technology. Thank God for video transmission! We were able to make a three-way call across worldwide time zones and see and talk to each other. We watched our granddaughter open her gifts, ooh and aah while ripping through paper, and play with one toy after another. If only technology could invent a way to give a hug.

I tried to focus on what I could be thankful for instead of focusing on our separations. I knew if I got into that mindset, depression would set in. As I counted my blessings, I realized none of our family members had been sick; we had arrived safely; and we were blessed with a method to communicate with each other. I couldn't complain.

The miles between us, and the days that pass until we can all be together again make me appreciate more than ever the family God has given me. Time on this earth is short, and the older I get, the more aware I am of how quickly those moments pass.

Covid was a hurdle we all had to jump. Many continue to do so. The hardships we encountered taught us to dig deeper into our resilience and find out what we are really made of. We learned some of the supplies we coveted weren't as necessary for life as we thought.

We also learned to focus on life, family, and friends more than on items on store shelves.

I hope our long-distance holidays will be fewer as the years go by, but nothing can take away the truth that no matter where we are, Christmas gave us God's Son — the best gift we could ever have.

31

Christmas in Bavaria

E. V. Sparrow

The cuckoo clock's tiny bird chirped six times as Hannah pulled a wool sweater over her head and long braid. She entered the kitchenette to double-check the 1981 Picturesque Castles wall calendar she'd purchased in Munich. She traced the week to December 24. *I was right, 7 A.M. Enough time to walk to work.* She spread apart the lace curtain panels covering the frosty apartment window and studied the cloudy sky veiling the crest of the Alps. "Not snowing — for now."

Her landlady, Mrs. Byers, would still be asleep, so she couldn't ask to use the phone to call for a ride to work. Hannah tugged on snow boots and snatched the brown, down parka and scarf off the peg by her door. Maybe the shop had repaired Josh's car, and he'd pick her up? She'd best hurry to their usual meeting place at the church across the lane. She tiptoed through the boarding house, past the other lodgers' doors, down three floors of carpeted stairs, and out the front door. Her breath froze in the air, and she pulled the scarf over her nose.

A snowplow turned the corner, past Hannah's apartment, and headed down the cobblestone street in front of the church. It sprayed snow in an arch next to the sidewalk, almost reaching the base of the tiny balcony off the kitchenette. This amount of snow was so mind-boggling that her family and friends in the States might not believe her.

She shielded her eyes against the glaring sun that cut between scattering clouds, adjusted her wool cap, and squinted upward to find the snowbank's crest. *There's the marker.*

"Almost thirty feet of snow? Good Lord."

"Talking to yourself again?" Josh, trekked toward her up the icy sidewalk sprinkled with sand. His hazel eyes crinkled above his scarf.

Hannah uncovered her face. "A sign of a brilliant imagination. I can't believe how much snow Garmisch has. I see you're without your car, which means I walk to work."

Josh chuckled. "Be thankful you're able to walk. Mainly because they've cleared the roads. That's what makes me thankful. German efficiency. You can take a bus." He planted a kiss on top of her head. "Good news . . . My car is ready. I pick it up from the shop this afternoon."

"Finally! Since you have the only car among our friends, you know the buses don't run this early. But now, we won't need public transportation anymore. — We can depend on you."

"Dependable me." He patted his chest. "Plus, we can go out for that Christmas Eve dinner I promised."

"*Danke*." Hannah bobbed a curtsy and stomped her feet to keep her circulation going. "Did the police find out who stole parts from your car or trashed it with beer and stuff?"

"Nope, but thieves sell stolen parts on the black market." Josh squeezed her shoulder. "So, I'll pick you up at 6:00 tonight, after I get Mike and Meg. It should still be light enough for you to see the frozen Eibsee with no sailboats on it." He wiggled his brows.

"The stunning lake without boats, *or* tourists for once. And a feast at the Färnhaus. I can't wait to write about my first Christmas in Bavaria."

Josh waved as he turned away. "*Auf Wiedersehen.*"

Hannah rearranged her scarf to cover her nose again before she trudged up the street to the ski rental shop. "All I've been doing is work, work, work in this winter wonderland."

* * *

In the dim lobby of the Färnhaus restaurant, a Christmas tree flickered with tiny, lighted red candles nestled within gold holders clipped to the branches. "They'd never allow us to do this back home.

Meg, isn't it the most beautiful tree you've ever seen? And there's the cranberry and popcorn garlands. Classic."

"Definitely. Once you've seen a German tree with real candles, it's disappointing to decorate one with light bulbs or anything fake."

The four friends feasted on roast pork loin, *spätzle*, and *blumenkohl* (cauliflower). They didn't order dessert because Meg's baked and iced gingerbread men cookies waited at Hannah's apartment.

Josh leaned toward Hannah. "By the joy in your eyes, I made an excellent choice for dinner here, right?"

She grinned. "Could be . . . . Now for the Eibsee. The rest of my gift."

* * *

Although the snowfall had begun again as they ate, Josh escorted the group of friends to the Eibsee in Grainau. He was right. There was enough twilight left to view the wide, dark, and thoroughly frozen lake. Hannah imagined ice-skating on it as she had done once in Yosemite, but ice-skating wasn't yet available.

On the return trip, Josh turned down a road that appeared clear, but was unplowed further on. The car got stuck against an object buried beneath the snow. He tried to reverse, and the chained tires spun out.

Everyone climbed out of the car and, in the deepening night, searched for the flashlight in the trunk and underneath the car seats.

Josh rummaged through the glove compartment. "It *was* here. I bet the thugs stole it when they broke in. I didn't notice it missing before."

The group pushed and shoved the car repeatedly, in many directions, but it seemed stuck in a hole and wouldn't budge.

"Can anyone see any houses?" Mike asked. "I think we're isolated."

"It's too dark to make out anything." Hannah listened for any sounds of humanity, but there was only the gentle plop of snowflakes.

Meg, Josh, and Mike discussed what to do, how to get help, or if they would need to spend the night in the car. Blankets were in the trunk, but was there enough fuel to run the heater overnight? Should they attempt walking back to the main road in the dark?

Hannah's heart pounded. *Stranded?* In the middle of nowhere? What should they do? The moonless sky created a snowy landscape difficult to discern, except for the darker blueish shapes of the Alps, cedars, and contours of a narrow ravine. "There's no one around to help. It's getting creepy. So still . . . and silent."

"Let's pray for wisdom on what to do here," Josh said. The group held hands in a circle, then asked God for protection and a way of escape from their dilemma.

"Amen." Hannah lifted her head and studied the landscape once more. Suddenly, a golden glow appeared in the darkness across the ravine. "What's that?"

Warm light spilled down the far hillside from a small church's open door. The gothic stained-glass windows sparkled like a kaleidoscope, and pinpoints of light spread out in front of the church.

"There's people!" Relief rushed through Hannah.

Several people lit candles and placed them in the snow near the church's gravestones. They created a scenic gold, teal, and midnight blue masterpiece.

"*Stille Nacht, heilige nacht,* (Silent Night, holy night)

Alles schlaft; einsam wacht . . . ." (All is calm; all is bright)

Hannah gasped. "That's *Silent Night!*"

Meg sang along in her perfect German, while the others joined in on the words they knew.

Chills spread up Hannah's arms. "It's glorious and soothing a capella . . . with their voices echoing around us." She clapped her gloved hands. "Best gift ever! We would've missed out on this if the car hadn't gotten stuck here."

The friends huddled together and murmured about God's perfect timing for them to experience the blessing of this mesmerizing song in the dark of night and during their predicament.

"Yup, it was soothing, but we're still stuck," Josh said. "Got an idea!" He opened the car door, activating the cab light and switched the headlamps on. Josh and Mike cupped their hands around their mouths and bellowed in German across the ravine, "Help! Help! We're stuck!"

They waved their arms over their heads while spotlighted in the bright beams.

Hannah frowned. "Can they hear? Oh, we heard *them*. Let's yell together on three."

Several little flames on the hillside bobbed together, then stilled. People yelled a request to dentify their exact location.

Josh replied with the turnoff he took.

The group of friends piled back into Josh's car, turned on the heater, and waited.

About fifteen minutes later, headlights blazed through the back window, and three people climbed out of a truck. They tied a rope to Josh's rear bumper, and everyone pushed from the front as the truck tugged his car backwards the way they had driven in from Grainau.

Hannah pondered the miraculous events while the truck towed them away from the vanishing, dreamlike scene. She turned to Josh. "Isn't it breathtaking how God always does the unexpected? First the manger, then the crucifixion, and then Jesus's resurrection. Nobody expected any of those."

"True," Josh agreed. "We also witnessed His masterful timing."

"Amen! God answered our prayers for escape, plus gave us an unexpected Christmas experience we'll never forget."

32

Fakeys!

Barb Fox

These will be perfect!" Melanie thought.

My mother-in-law, Melanie the master gardner, carefully selected the best-looking poinsettias and placed them in her cart. The festive plants would serve as holiday table decorations and door prizes for the church's Christmas dinner.

As she checked out, she gently removed the flowers from her cart and asked the clerk to help her place a bag over each pot to protect them from the frigid Ohio weather. The clerk looked a little annoyed but complied with the request.

When Melanie got home, she uncovered her treasures, situated them to receive indirect sunlight, and watered them regularly. On the day of the Christmas party, she wrapped them up again to transport them to the church. She noticed water pooling at the bottom of the red foil wrappers, so she took extra care not to spill them.

At the church, she placed one poinsettia on each table, then pressed her finger into the last pot to see if it needed more water. Her finger hit hard plastic instead of soft soil. Confused, she looked more closely.

"They're fakeys!" she yelped.

When it came time to award the door prizes, she warned everyone to be careful not to spill the water she'd poured into the artificial plants. The crowd roared with laughter because the master gardener, had been deceived.

I can't laugh too loudly because sometimes I am deceived, too. My problem isn't watering artificial flowers, though; it's watering activities instead of spiritual growth in my life.

Be doers of the word, and not hearers only, deceiving yourselves.

(James 1:22 esv)

Is it enough to simply listen to a sermon on Sunday or read my Bible daily? Do these activities mean my faith is thriving?

First, I need to check the soil. Jesus told a parable that referred to the heart as soil (Matthew 13).

- The first type of soil is packed earth, it refers to a heart so hard that God's truths do not penetrate, and so nothing ever begins to grow.

- The second, rocky soil, refers to a heart that develops shallow roots. God's truths start to take root, but when trials come, I revert back to my old nature because I never allowed the truths to reach down to my character, thoughts, and motives.

- The third type, thorny soil, refers to a heart that allows worldly priorities to take precedence over God's priorities — choosing to make money or advance in my career over living righteously before God, for instance.

- The good soil welcomes God's truth and allows it to grow. Do I welcome God's seeds of change in my life?

  For example, when I sense Him urging me to forgive someone, do I resist emphatically or respond enthusiastically? When I see a need, do I look for ways to help, or do I push the thought to the back of my mind? If I hesitate, I might be deceiving myself into thinking that knowledge about the Bible is spiritual growth. Yet Scripture tells us faith without works is dead.

  Second, I should examine whether my faith exhibits characteristics of life. Live things grow and change. A live poinsettia will grow new leaves, allow old leaves to dry up and fall off, and grow a stronger root system. If I am alive in Christ, I should see similar changes in my life. I will exhibit new fruit (like kindness), I will allow bad habits to die, and I will persevere through difficult seasons without wilting.

Live plants reproduce. New poinsettias grow from either a cutting or from the seeds of a mature poinsettia. If I am a living branch of Christ, then I will reproduce, creating spiritual children who then create spiritual children. Next Christmas I should be able to look back and celebrate how cuttings from my life served as catalysts for the spiritual growth of other people.

Next, I can look at the fruit. Mark 4:20 says that when God's Word is planted in good soil, it produces a crop that yields thirty, sixty, or a hundred times what was sown. I want God's abundance in my life to be as exuberant as Christmas decorations, church sanctuaries filled with festive poinsettias, green holly bejeweled with red berries, Christmas trees filling the air with their lovely scent. Attractive. Delightful. Bringing joy into people's lives.

Is my life bringing beauty to God's kingdom? Are blossoms of self-control and love thriving? Am I harvesting greater self-control and perseverance?

> *Faith by itself, if it does not have works, is dead.*
> James 2:17 ESV

Choosing What to Water

I don't want to be fakey. I want to be authentic. I may think I'm being watered by listening to podcasts and doing Bible studies, but the living water will run off if my heart is hard. In that case, I would only be a hearer who is deceiving myself. God wants me to trust Him and follow His lead.

Melanie's story reminded me how silly it is to water fake plants. Yet, I've been known to do that. I encounter an irritating co-worker who rubs me the wrong way, so I paint on a fake smile. With lots of effort, I may be able to maintain that fake smile for a few minutes, but what good does that do? Instead, I can use the same amount of energy to pray for her and ask God to soften my heart. When I begin to see her as God sees her, I will naturally treat her with kindness and love.

As we decide what to nurture in our lives, let's not be deceived. Let's choose to water truth and righteousness.

Confess and Move On

When I realize I've been deceiving myself, I sometimes hide from the truth or even try to convince other people to believe the same deception. I like Melanie's approach better. Admit it. Laugh or cry, but don't hide it. Tell trusted friends how it happened and what you learned from it.

God gives us this advice: *Confess your sins to one another and pray for one another, that you may be healed"* (James 5:16 ESV).

Door Prize

The one who looks into the perfect law, the law of liberty, and perseveres, being no hearer who forgets but a doer who acts, he will be blessed in his doing. (James 1:25 ESV)

A few of Melanie's friends received silk poinsettias as door prizes. As friends of God, we welcome the more excellent gift of lifelong blessings as He transforms us from the inside out. God rejoices when we allow Him to perform good works through us, using our living faith to bring beauty, joy, and hope into the world.

When I see poinsettias this Christmas, I'll chuckle as I remember my mother-in-law's story, and then I'll pray for you and me.

May our actions prove we're not fakeys. Thanks be to God for enabling us to be the real thing.

33

The Christmas Tree Branches

AimeeAnn Blythe

As a young girl, I couldn't wait for November every year. Just before Thanksgiving merchants would begin setting up their lots for Christmas tree sales and I knew the smells of Christmas would soon follow.

A couple of times a week Mom and I would go to the grocery stores next to these lots. When we got out of the car, the aromatic scent of the spruce, pine, and fir trees wafted through the air.

All I could think about as we entered the grocery store was when we could finally buy our Christmas tree. Each time I asked the same question, "Can we buy one today?" What I didn't know then was Mom was waiting for just the right time to purchase our tree so it might last past Christmas and possibly to New Year's Day.

I remember one year, each time I asked, Mom was patient, saying, "Not today." The odd thing was, we stopped by the lot (now filled with Christmas trees) each time we exited the grocery store. She went over to the person in charge, said something, and he gave her the scrap branches cut from the bottom of trees. There were only a few branches but their scent filled the car on the way home.

Why would anyone want those, I wondered?

At home, Mom placed the branches in water in an old metal bucket on the carport. I was still in school before the much-anticipated Christmas break and never noticed the changing number of branches in the container.

It wasn't until I happened to be standing next to her at church one Sunday that I learned what Mom was doing with those scraps. Sometime during the school day, she would make something simple with the greenery and place a small votive candle and glass holder in the center. Before I got home, she delivered the petite arrangement — along with an assortment of sugar cookies, Kringle (a pastry), or pieces of pie she had baked — to an older member of our congregation.

Because of their advanced age, these people didn't bake or decorate for Christmas much anymore. I'm sure they thanked Mom for the kindness at the time of delivery, but it was only when the woman told Mom that day just how much she appreciated the arrangement and baked goods that I realized what Mom was doing. The woman said the scents of the greenery and candle took her back to her family Christmases, which she had not experienced in several years. She had even shared some of the cookies with her neighbor.

The day finally came when we picked out a Christmas tree. I don't remember what variety it was, only that it smelled like the holidays. That Christmas, I learned more about the spirit of Christmas and giving to others.

Now many years later, I marvel at the warm, fuzzy feeling that comes over me when I see a Christmas tree lot and the scents remind me of Mom's ability and creativity to bring love and happiness to others during the holiday season.

Thanks for the memory, Mom.

34

Home for Christmas Again

Joann Claypoole

H ome. It's where the love light gleams —"

The truth of those words cut deep last Christmas. Several members of our immediate family didn't join us for our usual holiday celebrations. The only visual communication: via Zoom or FaceTime. For the first time in thirty-something years, I didn't cook a ton of food, and we exchanged simple gifts two days before Christmas.

Two of our four sons donned surgical masks. One pulled a black mask up around his forehead. My husband laughed and said, "Are you trying to resemble Zorro?" Our youngest son, Noah, gave me a puny, masked hug. "I'm sorry no one's coming tomorrow, Mom. I know how you love everyone to be together on Christmas Eve, but everyone's staying home for Christmas this year."

The only problem? They weren't *home* with us.

My husband packed our Jeep early the next morning and we headed north to our cabin in the mountains.

It seldom snows on Christmas in our remote western North Carolina town. The Weather Channel's prediction called for rain, not eight inches of snow. We arrived from Florida a half-hour before the storm hit with little warning.

"See, Baby," my husband Dennis said, "God gave you lots of snow this Christmas Eve. It's His way of letting you know He loves you. He knows how much you miss the kids. Everything will be better next year. We'll all be together — right here in our tiny house."

"Home for Christmas? Here? Fulltime?" The thought of no more nine-hour drives north or south every few weeks thrilled me. And no more living in the furnace we call Florida boggled my mind. "Yay!"

"Now do you feel better about this holiday season being so different from our usual fantastic chaos?" He handed me a small gift box wrapped in red paper, and winked at me when I held up the beautiful necklace.

"I love it."

A few days later, we celebrated New Year's Eve with bowls of chili and glasses of wine by the fireside.

"It's crazy," I said. "One of my fondest dreams will come true, but the world is still in the middle of a viral nightmare." The realization we'd soon live in North Carolina fulltime sent my heart soaring, while the mom in me worried about our family in Florida.

I retired from the stylist/colorist business two months later, in early March. In some ways, living with a world-wide pandemic for over a year made the move easier. After all, Dennis' job wouldn't have gone remote if the dreadful pandemic hadn't spread and then recently resurged again.

Isn't it weird how some curses can also bring blessings?

Changes in the way businesses operated happened over the course of several months. Doors that had been sealed shut for years now flew open so Dennis could work from home. He slowed way down. And I knew that was a good thing — especially since he'd suffered a heart attack in January 2020.

"I'll still miss the children," I said, reminding myself how thankful I was to know our sons and their families promised to visit during the summer. "Wouldn't it be great if everyone moved here? Then we could all be together next Christmas. That would be my only Christmas wish."

"Sounds a bit unrealistic."

"That's why they're called Christmas wishes."

I envisioned our cabin bursting at the seams with kids and dogs running amuck. Snow-covered mountains added to the ideal scene.

Children huddled beside the tree listening to the age-old story. Laughter, song, and the intoxicating scent of Christmas cookies filling the air. All eyes bright and gazing at the fireplace as logs crackled and embers glowed.

Dennis' nudge rattled me out of the fantastic daydream. He laughed and leaned in to hug me. "I'm not so sure that wish will ever come true. Let's take it one day at a time."

"It may take a few months to organize our own move from Florida," he said, and although his wisdom usually comforted me, I let out a sigh.

"Packing a huge house is so tedious. I wish we could blink and get on with living in the mountains. If I can't see our grandchildren often, we might as well be in Siberia."

A few months passed. We sold our Florida home before the daffodils waned in late spring. Our long-held dream became reality.

Thankful to be preparing my North Carolina hillside garden for summer, I took off my baseball cap, and for a moment I let the sun caress my face. Tears streamed down my cheeks as memories of past holidays flooded my mind.

God, please let this crazy pandemic end. I pray for the day life will be normal again.

It had been too long since our kids and grandchildren had come to visit us. They'd loved visiting the cabin for seasonal celebrations since we purchased the vacation getaway in 2016. The children enjoyed swimming in the lake, boating, tubing, hiking, and sledding — and trekking through my woodland garden too. They also adored the decorations and lights we placed on the hillside every Christmas.

My husband joined in all the preparations. "I can't wait to see them either." He smiled and wiped a tear from his eye, too. I grabbed handsful of dirt and planted flowers while he flung three yards of mulch up the hillside.

After a while, I looked at my husband and said, "Thank God it's almost over."

"So, we're done planting flowers? The look on his face was priceless. "I thought you loved gardening and never had enough roses?"

"I meant the pandemic, silly. It's like waking from a bad dream. Soon everything will be back to normal."

"Maybe not so soon—"

"Anyway," I said, "I hope you're not right. Christmas is only a few months away.

After several weeks of long-awaited memorable family visits this scorching summer, I focused my thoughts on God's grace, His unimaginable love for us, and how He's with us throughout life's challenges and storms. How strength comes from trials. And how my strength is only in Him. He's the giver of all our seasons. Good, bad, and ugly. He's also the giver of life.

Labor Day was only a few weeks away when I pointed out several people wearing masks while Dennis and I shopped at our local grocery store. "What's up with all the masks again?"

"Haven't watched the news lately?"

"I hate the news."

"Huh?"

"My mother always said, 'No news is good news.'"

"Your mom was right," Dennis said as he handed me the TV remote when we arrived home.

"Oh no!"

For a moment, my thoughts turned inward. How could this be happening again? And right before the holidays?

I reminded myself about the incredible news we'd recently received from one of our sons. "'We're looking at houses online, Mom. We're moving up there before Christmas.'"

This amazing blessing came from out of nowhere. See, some Christmas wishes really do come true. It reinforced the fact that no matter what we'd faced throughout the years, we'd always counted on God, one another . . . and yes, celebrating holidays together, too.

Although things have changed since the Covid-19 dilemma started, and the fate of future gatherings grips a fearful world yet again, I believe God's plan is much bigger than this bug. His ways are so much higher. Only He knows all our tomorrows. So, with my thoughts on the manger, I will trust in Him today.

It came upon a midnight clear . . . .

Alone and unsure of the future, the newlywed couple awaited the birth of Jesus, God's Son, in a lowly stable. The company of livestock and unseen angels stood in place of family and friends. When I think about their reality and the raw truth of the story, a different perspective of any present loneliness calms my soul.

While I miss my sons and grandchildren, I imagine how Mary and Joseph's weariness and emptiness of going it alone through such unforeseen circumstances could have taken its toll. Instead, their season of solitude brought forth peace, joy, contentment, and deeper love. I'm thankful for their example as we make the most of possibly celebrating another Christmas minus the parties, crowded festivals, or lavish feasts.

Home for Christmas has taken on a new interpretation since last year's unusual holiday season when we were forced into quiet mode. The true meaning of Christmas, however, remains the same and rings ever clearer this year.

It's time to remember and share the gift of hope. Whether it be via Zoom, Google Meet, or FaceTime — the essence of the message will never change: We're not alone, at Christmas or any other day of the year, God is with us.

About the Authors

AimeeAnn Blythe lives in rural western Tennessee with her husband, squirrels, rabbits, raccoons and deer all doing hilarious, crazy things. Visit her website https://aimeeannblythe.com.

Susan Brehmer, an encourager and Bible enthusiast, believes treasure is found in the Word of God and time with Jesus sheds light on scripture. She loves to lead others into worship and through the life-changing Word of God. Host of the *Encouraging Voice Podcast*, she writes worship songs, devotional articles for the *Christian Journal* (thechristianjournal. org), and devotions for *Pathways to God*. Her original songs, as well as Bible insights, can be found on her website at www.SusanBrehmer.com.

Jeanetta Chrystie, ThD, PhD whose published works include more than 800 magazine articles, 150 newspaper columns, 2 poetry chapbooks, singly published poems, and 2 college textbooks, has written part-time for more than 40 years. She has also contributed to several anthologies, including *Chicken Soup for the Soul: The Miracle of Love* and *Abba's Answers*.

Learn more about Dr. Chrystie at www.ClearGlassView.com. Connect with Jeanetta on Twitter: @ClearGlassView, LinkedIn: Jeanetta-Chrystie, and Pinterest: Jchrystie."

Joann Claypoole is an author, speaker, and former spa-girl entrepreneur. She's a wife, mother of four sons, "Numi" to four grandchildren, doggie-mom of two. The award-winning author of *The Gardener's Helpers* (ages 5-9) would rather be writing, hiking in the mountains, or inviting deer and other wildlife to stay for dinner near her western North Carolina writing retreat.

Elberta Clinton, a third-generation Missouri Ozarks native, is an only child who grew up first watching and then helping her mother bake. Giving their baked goods away was important then and continues to be so now. The high-schooler, described in her story as the sentimental "keeper of the one-handle rolling pin," now attends East Coast university. A special item she took with her was a batch of homemade "friend maker" cookies from her grandmother.

Diana C. Derringer is an award-winning writer and author of *Beyond Bethlehem and Calvary: 12 Dramas for Christmas, Easter, and More!* More than 1,000 of her articles, devotions, dramas, planning guides, Bible studies, and poems appear in over 70 publications, including several anthologies. In addition, Diana writes radio drama for Christ to the World Ministries. Her adventures as a social worker, adjunct professor, youth Sunday school teacher, and friendship family for international university students supply a constant flow of writing ideas. For a free copy of Diana's "Words of Hope for Days That Hurt" and her weekly *Words, Wit, and Wisdom: Life Lessons from English Expressions*, join her mailing list at https://dianaderringer.com.

Jennifer A. Doss resides in Indiana with her husband and four children. Each day, she strives to draw closer to God and find ways to inspire and encourage others. Her other joys include spending time outdoors in the shade and hanging out with her family. Any success or achievements are from the Lord and all credit goes to Him.

Barb Fox is a teacher at heart. She loves motivating others to dig deeper into the Word. Research scientist by day and Christian author by night, she thanks God for weekends and a husband who keeps life fun even when she sometimes gets a bit too serious.

Constance Gilbert is an inspirational short-story writer. Music and books have been a major part of her life since age 7. She knits and colors to stimulate her little gray (brain) cells, but studying Scripture is her passion. Connie, a retired RN has many experiences plus the nearby Cascade Mountains and three grandkids to inspire her. Her most recently published story "Olivia, the Fierce" shows her love of taking everyday things and happenings to a deeper level.

Jean Matthew Hall lives in LaGrange, Kentucky with her old-lady dog, Sophie. Jean writes poems, stories, articles and picture books while Sophie naps. Her first picture book, *God's Blessings of Fall,* was released by Little Lamb Books in September 2019. Her second picture book is set to release in 2022. When not enjoying time with family (eight gorgeous grandkids) and church, Jean is immersed in children's picture books — reading, studying, reviewing, and writing them. She is a member of the SCBWI, Word Weavers International, Write2Ignite and Kentucky Christian Writers. Jean has been a Christian for more than 50 years. You can learn more about her at her website and blog www.jeanmatthewhall. com. Find her on FaceBook at JeanMatthewHallAuthor and on Twitter at Jean_Hall. Check out her Boards on Pinterests at JeanMatthew_Hall.

Bonnie Lasley Harker is a mother, grandmother, and great-grand-mother. She loves God, her family, and her poetry. Her works also include devotionals. She claims poetry came to her as a gift from God during a pruning time, as spoken of by Jesus in John 15:5. However, the gift has continued for 23 years. Bonnie never knows when inspiration will come. She testifies to the fact God triggers it with a couple of phrases, and leaves the rest in her hands.

Lydia E. Harris has been married to her college sweetheart, Milt, for more than 50 years. She enjoys spending time with her family, which includes two married children and five grandchildren aged 11 to 22. She is the author of two books for grandparents: *Preparing My Heart for Grandparenting: for Grandparents at Any Stage of the Journey* and *In the Kitchen with Grandma: Stirring Up Tasty Memories Together*. With a master's degree in Home Economics, Lydia creates and tests recipes with her grandchildren for Focus on the Family children's magazines. She also pens the column "A Cup of Tea with Lydia," which is published in the US and Canada. It's no wonder she is known as "Grandma Tea."

Shirl Hart walked into an airplane propeller at age sixteen. Disfigured and without family support she worked her way through college then married the most eligible bachelor in Des Moines, Iowa. Together she and Tom lived in the country, raised three sons, then moved to Florida to care for his widowed mother. In later years they ran a care-giving business. During that time she located and met her two sisters.

Melissa Henderson, an award-winning author, writes inspirational messages sometimes laced with a bit of humor. With stories in books and magazines, devotionals, and articles, Melissa hopes to encourage readers. Her family motto is "It's Always a Story With the Hendersons." Follow her at http://www.melissaghenderson.com and on social media.

Judith Victoria Hensley, a retired middle school teacher, weekly newspaper columnist, and author resides in the mountains of southeastern Kentucky. She writes for the Christian market, middle grade chapter books, and Appalachian culture. She is working on the eighth book in the Christian women's anthology *Warrior Women Series – Light in the Darkness*.

Helen L. Hoover and her husband are retired and live in the Ozark Mountains of south-central Missouri. Sewing, reading, knitting, traveling, tending her flower gardens, and helping her husband with home repair occupy her time. Word Aflame Publishing, *The Secret Place, Word Action Publication, The Quiet Hour, The Lutheran Digest, Light and Life Communications, Chicken Soup for the Soul,* and *Victory in Grace* have published her devotionals and personal articles. Visits with their two living children, grandchildren, and great-grandchildren are treasured.

Rita Klundt became an author, speaker and story collector after 30 years as a registered professional nurse. Her first book, *Goliath's Mountain,* tells a poignant and tragic love story giving readers a view into the heart of a woman touched by mental illness and suicide. Rita's passion for true and transparent stories has led her to collect more stories than she can write or tell in her lifetime. She collaborated with 26 friends to compile and publish *Real Life Real Ladies: Short Stories from the Pew,* the first in a series of books. Rita and her husband live in central Illinois. They enjoy travel and are excited about where this stage of life and story collecting is taking them. Connect with Rita or watch for more great stories at www.ritaklundt.com.

Barbara Latta, a true southerner, is transplanted from Arkansas to Georgia. She writes a monthly column in her local newspaper and contributes to devotional websites, online magazines, and has stories in several anthologies. She is the author of *God's Maps, Stories of Inspiration and Direction for Motorcycle Riders.* She enjoys traveling with her Harleyriding prince taking in the creativity of nature. Drinking coffee on the patio while the sun comes up is her favorite time of day. Barbara shares about walking in grace and thriving in hope on her blog, *Navigating Life's Curves*, at www.barbaralatta.blogspot.com. She cherishes her role in life as a wife, a mom, mother-in-law, and Mimi to one granddaughter.

Diana Leagh Matthews has a heart for sharing God's love. Whether writing, singing, researching history, or working with seniors in nursing homes, she longs to shine for Christ. She has contributed to many of the *Moments* books, and is the author of *90 Breath Prayers for the Healthcare Professional, 90 Breath Prayers for the Caregiver, the 90 Breath Prayer Journal*, and the upcoming *90 Breath Prayers for those with Health Challenges*. Diana shares hymn stories on her blog at DianaLeaghMatthews.com and hymn-votions on social media. She resides in South Carolina.

Terri R. Miller is an award-winning writer and an aspiring novelist. Her articles have been published in magazines and two other anthologies, *Pandemic Moments* and *When Life Gives You Lemons: Short Stories to Make You Smile*. On her blog, *Life Is Moments* (Lifeismoments. blog), Terri writes about everyday moments that connect us to God, each other, and ourselves. She enjoys birdwatching, gardening, cooking, and small-town life in Alabama with her husband, David.

Lynn Mosher has had her socked feet firmly planted in the Midwest since she drew her first breath. She is the keeper of a secret recipe for barbecue sauce, which she may share if you bribe her with enough chocolate.

Though an upheaval of illness has stalked her for many years, her deepest passion is sharing her devotionals, inspirational stories, and graphics on social media, fulfilling God's call on her life to encourage others and glorify the Lord with her writing. Subscribe to her weekly devotional, *Letters from the Couch*, at http://eepurl.com/b5n-Pf.

Suzanne D. Nichols grew up in Gulf Breeze, Florida where, during a high school composition class, she discovered the rewarding discipline of writing. Through the years, she has found creative expression in almost every genre of the printed word. She especially enjoys blending words and art in ways that can both delight and challenge the observer.

Suzanne is published in seven books of Grace Publishing's *Short and Sweet* series, is co-author of *COFFEE with God, Volumes 1 and 2*, a contributor to *Day by Day: 40 Devotionals for Writers & Creative Types*, and is a 2021 Selah Awards recipient.

Suzanne lives in Hartselle, Alabama with her husband of 45 years. They have 3 children and 9 grandchildren who live much too far away.

Jane Owen is a freelance writer and retired teacher who lives with her husband, Ron, in Salt Lake City. She is grateful to the Lord to live close to their three grandchildren, who create lots of memory-making moments. Her short stories, devotionals, and feature articles have appeared in *The Upper Room*, Guidepost Books, St. Martin's Press, Bethany House Publishing, Worthy Media, Inc., Standard Publishing, and Grace Publishing's 2020 *Christmas Stories* anthology. Contact her at ladyjaneut@aol.com

Sue Rice, a Kent State University graduate, is retired from a career in Human Resources Management. She enjoys writing and has been published in a number of magazines including *Guideposts, GRAND,* and *The Liguorian*. She also enjoys hiking with her dog, Buddy. (They have logged over 1,000 miles.) Sue has worked with students from around the world and currently teaches ESL. She is working on a book about people's memories of spending time with their grandparents.

Beverly Robertson is a retired elementary instructional aide. She completed a course from the Institute of Children's Literature and earned an associate degree from Delta College. She networks and hones her writing skills as a member of American Christian Fiction Writers. For her Presbyterian women's group, she presented monthly lessons on different women of the Bible. Beverly is the author of *Bible Brides: Trials and Triumphs*. She lives in Michigan and is married with a daughter, stepson, five grandchildren and four great-grandchildren.

Robert B. Robeson has been published 930 times in 330 publications in 130 countries. This includes the *Reader's Digest, Positive Living, Soldier of Fortune, Logbook, Writer's Digest, Frontier Airline Magazine, Chicken Soup for the Soul, War Cry* and *Newsday*. His work has also been featured in 67 anthologies. Upon completing a 27 1/2-year career on three continents, he retired from the U.S. Army as a lieutenant colonel. Nineteen of those years were spent as a helicopter medical evacuation pilot. After his military retirement, he worked as a newspaper managing editor and columnist. He holds a BA in English from the University of Maryland, College Park, has completed extensive undergraduate and graduate work in journalism at the University of Nebraska, Lincoln, and is a professional (life) member of the National Writers Association, VFW, Dustoff Association, and the Distinguished Flying Cross Society. He lives in Lincoln, Nebraska with Phyllis, his wife of 53 years.

E.V. Sparrow believes you will encounter the unexpected when God works in people of fragile faith. Many of her 13 published short stories stem from her experiences overseas, witnessing God's grace and interest in people, and of His supernatural power. Her newest project is her debut, historical fiction novel. She is a member of Inspire Christian Writers and recently won second place in their Flash Fiction contest. She joined ACFW (American Christian Fiction Writers) after moving to North Carolina in 2021.

The most challenging job E.V. held was working for a non-profit program helping the elderly, homeless, and mentally ill population in Sacramento, California.

A Christian for 46 years, she's led prayer teams and small groups in Divorce Care, Women's, and Singles' Ministries, and sang with a worship team. She also served on short-term mission trips.

When she isn't writing or illustrating, she enjoys spending time with her husband and six grandchildren. Her favorite activities are hiking and kayaking.

Marv Stone is a software engineer sneaking dangerously close to 60. He and his wonderful wife of nearly 30 years, who is a retired nurse, have a 24-year-old son who is a worship leader and seminary student. Marv works from his home in a small town in north Mississippi. He loves teaching Sunday School, writing short stories, and playing with Annabelle, the 5-year-old mixed-breed dog his son swears is his replacement! Marv is an enthusiastic reader and thanks his mother for all those hours in the public library during summer breaks. It was her love for books that taught him to read and inspired him to write.

Mel Tavares has a unique background that makes her relatable to people from all walks of life. She is passionate about equipping people to thrive in a life of purpose and passion. She has been mentoring, counseling, and encouraging people (particularly women) for over 30 years — sometimes over a cup of coffee, sometimes through the printed page, and sometimes in person to groups. Regardless of the method, her message is the same: "Rise up and be all you were created to be!" Mel holds a Doctorate of Ministry in Pastoral Care and Counseling.

An award-winning author with four books, Mel is also a contributing writer to several works including DaySpring's *Sweet Tea for the Soul: Comfort for Grieving Hearts*. Her articles can be found online in many locations including CBN, Inspiration Ministries, *Christian Women Living* magazine, and *Inkspirations*. She also appears on PJNET and several podcasts.

You'll likely find her at her local church serving on staff, in her writing studio, or in the kitchen whipping up dinner for her growing blended family of seven kids and ten grands. If you still can't find her, check the front porch. She's often seen there sipping a cup of coffee. And if not there either, it is likely she's somewhere along the Connecticut Shoreline catching waves or a sunset with her beloved hubby, Joe.

Joy S. Taylor is the daughter of a coal miner's daughter, sister to three twins, mother of five, grandmother of ten-and-counting. Her work days were spent using the Master of Science in Accounting degree she earned at the age of, well, greater than 40. She led a divorce recovery support group sponsored by her church, and spent more than a decade in leadership roles for Celebrate Recovery. Now retired, she concentrates on writing, yet devotes some of her time to volunteering for Care Net. With several of her poems published in separate compilations by the International Library of Poetry, she has two of her own compilations published —*Findings: My Journey to Joy* and *Finding Brighter Days*. Joy currently lives in Indiana and writes from the peace of her beloved hickory grove.

Bill Tinsley, husband, father, grandfather, and great-grandfather, makes his home in Port Orange, Florida with Donna, his wife of 41 years. He chooses to be called a Brother in the Body of Christ. Bill pastored Coastland Agape in Melbourne, Florida and is owner of Gator Construction of Central Florida, Inc.

Donna Collins Tinsley, wife, mother, grandmother, and great-grandmother, lives in Port Orange, Florida. Her work has been included in several magazines and book compilations. You can find her on Facebook, at http://thornrose7.blogspot.com/ or join Somebody's Mother Online Prayer Support Group on Facebook. You may email Donna at thornrose7@aol.com.

Diana L. Walters lives in Chattanooga, Tennessee with her husband. Together they develop ministry materials for people with dementia. At 74, she continues to work part-time enriching lives at a retirement community. She gardens and writes in her spare time. Diana has been published in *Chicken Soup for the Soul* books, *The Upper Room*, and other devotional publications.

Lynn U. Watson's first published writing, news about her Brownie troop, appeared in the *Milford* [Illinois] *Herald,* when she was seven years old. She is the author of *Cinnamah-Brosia's Inspirational Collection for Women.* Two of Lynn's stories have appeared in a previous *Divine Moments* anthology.

The great-great-granddaughter of a German baron, she has used a snippet of her family's story to inspire her fiction-writing journey.

Married since 1973, Lynn and her husband, Steve, fill their Bartlett, Tennessee, home with handmade treasures and lots of love for friends and family, and especially their five beautiful grandchildren. Aromas of freshly-baked bread frequently waft from her kitchen. Jasmine, the resident feline, runs the place.

Read more about Lynn's stories at LynnUWatson.com. Connect via Instagram @LynnUWatson.

Lori Ann Wood lives in beautiful Bentonville, Arkansas, with her husband, the love of her life whom she found in 9th grade. She is mom to three great young adults, one amazing son-in-law, and a miniature dachshund named Pearl.

Lori Ann serves as founding leader of the Parenting Education Ministry at the Church of Christ in Bentonville. She also serves as

WomenHeart Champion Community Educator for Arkansas and American Heart Association Ambassador. Lori Ann's work has been published in numerous print and online venues, including *Heart Insight, The Christian Century, Just Between Us, The Joyful Life, Bella Grace, Sweet to the Soul FAITH Magazine,* Pepperdine University Press, and yahoo.com.

Having discovered a serious heart condition almost too late, Lori Ann writes to encourage others to find joy in the divine detours of life. Read more from her at loriannwood.com.

CPSIA information can be obtained
at www.ICGtesting.com
Printed in the USA
LVHW011134270921
698786LV00004B/10